Concealed Carry Basics-

2017 Illinois Edition

By

Mike Keleher

DISCLAIMER

Statutes appear in this edition, but information in this book is not to be considered to be legal advice for specific cases. The author disclaims any and all liabilities, losses, costs, claims, suits or actions arising from the book, the use of information found in the book or any claim a particular action taken as a result of reading the book. Students and gun owners are responsible for knowing the law as it applies to their own situations and obtaining legal advice from their own attorneys, the local State's Attorneys Office or the Attorney General's Office. Laws are subject to change and interpretation and the reader's lawyer or prosecutors would be able to fully research legal topics and render an opinion on how it applies to any set of circumstances. The information in this book is for educational and instructional purpose only and is intended for incorporation into an Illinois state certified training curriculum. The book is not a substitute for the state mandated training required under 430 Illinois Compiled Statutes 66 (et al).

ISBN: 978-1-365-67760-1

Dedication: To those who have waited so long to exercise their rights in a lawful manner. Illinois is the last state in the nation to allow Concealed Carry Licenses.

Somewhere along the way we lost sight of the fact that it is criminals who should be punished-not the law abiding public. Criminals don't follow the law, no matter how well-meaning or strenuously they are written.

Second Amendment to the U.S. Constitution

"A well regulated Militia, being necessary to the security of a free State, the right of the people to keep and bear Arms, shall not be infringed."

CONTENTS

CHAPTER ONE
THE ILLINOIS CONCEALED CARRY LICENSE
COURSE DESCRIPTION

The state of Illinois is the last state in the nation to allow Concealed Carry Licenses and has a rigorous requirement of topics which an applicant must be trained in prior to applying to for a state permit. All such training must be covered by a state certified Concealed Carry instructor and the student must complete all mandated training (either 8 hours or 16 hours) and pass a shooting test. The state allows the instructor to add to the topics, the details and even additional length of the training if they desire, but the instructor cannot drop below the required curriculum and minimum length of time for instruction. The applicant may (not must) also submit a set of fingerprints via a state certified vendor and a recent photograph taken within the last 30 days.

The state mandated training topics include safety with firearms, marksmanship, cleaning, loading and unloading weapons, state and federal laws which apply to the carry of concealed weapons, and demonstrated weapons handling which includes at least one close range 30 round course of fire shot in the instructor's presence on a state mandated B-27 target.

All applicants must be at least twenty one years old, have a state driver's license and state residents must have a valid Illinois Firearms Owners Identification card (FOID card). They may not be a person prohibited via federal laws from possessing or receiving a firearm (example- Convicted Felon). They cannot have been convicted in any state of even a misdemeanor involving violence or the threat of violence or force within the previous five years. They cannot have two or more violations of Driving Under the Influence (DUI) with alcohol, drugs or a combination within the last five years. Applicants also cannot have pending arrest warrants, be pending prosecution or been sentenced to in-patient (residential type) or court ordered drug or alcohol treatment within the last five years.

Any violations of these conditions will result in the state declining to issue a concealed weapons carry License even if the applicant took all of the mandated firearms training paid the fees and provided all of the other necessary data for the application process.

The cost of the Concealed Carry License is $150 and the state permit is valid for five years. The cost of the pre-licensing training via an instructor and fingerprint submission are additional costs which are not covered in the $150 state license fee.

Per their website, the Illinois State Police state they received 78,000 Concealed Carry License applications in the first year of eligibility, 2014.

Open Carry

Illinois has no statute allowing the state wide open or unconcealed carry of a firearm in public. Now that the Concealed Carry License law has been passed there is interest in an Open Carry law, but with this would require years of advocacy and legislative effort.

If you are going to carry a firearm on your person or in your automobile in the state of Illinois it must be concealed at all times and you must have both an Illinois Concealed Carry License and an Illinois FOID card in your possession.

FOID Card requirement.

Illinois has a requirement that any adult resident who wants to purchase or possess firearms and ammunition must first obtain an Illinois Firearms Owners Identification Card (FOID). This law was put into place in 1968 as a way to identify individuals who have passed a criminal history background check with the state. The card must be maintained on their person while possessing, moving or purchasing guns and ammunition. No other state in the nation has a similar statue, and the law requiring the FOID has survived court challenges to its constitutionality as a limit on the right to keep and bear arms.

A FOID card is not, and has never been a License for concealed carry, yet a citizen must have a FOID card issued in their name on their person if they are in possession of a firearm with their Concealed Carry License. The FOID card merely identifies the owner as being eligible to possess guns and ammunition and the Concealed Carry License allows the actual carry of those items. Non-residents do not have to obtain a FOID card.

FOID cards are issued by the Illinois State Police and require sending in a completed application, a photo and a fee of $10. The cards are valid for ten years. The application can be picked up locally at State Police stations, in gun stores or other stores where firearms are sold or the form may be downloaded from the ISP web site at: http://www.isp.state.il.us/foid/foidapp.cfm.

The state police website cautions applicants to apply early and expect delays as potential gun owners have been inundating the ISP for FOID card applications. America has experienced a groundswell of firearms and ammunition purchases and Illinois is no exception. In Jan 2013 the ISP had 61,172 FOID applications-that was double the amount received in 2012.

Additional information about the FOID card process can be accessed via the ISP website: http://www.isp.state.il.us/foid/foidapp.cfm.

CHAPTER TWO
FREQUENTLY ASKED QUESTIONS ABOUT THE ILLINOIS CONCEALED CARRY LICENSE

The Illinois State Police Website is the portal of entry for applying for the state license and it has a large amount of useful information an applicant can access including Frequently Asked Questions about the license and the application process via
https://www.ispfsb.com/Public/Faq.aspx

Some of the information listed include questions and answers like:

"How long does the application take to get issued?"
The state must make a determination and notification within 90 days of receipt. If fingerprints are not submitted it may take an additional 30 days for the process to be completed.

"Where can fingerprints be taken/submitted?"
You must use LiveScan digital fingerprint submissions via a state certified vendor. Any non-state certified vendor submissions will be rejected. The state provides a list of the certified vendors via
https://www.idfpr.com/LicenseLookUP/fingerprintlist.asp

"What type of firearm may be carried with a Concealed Carry License?"
The state says it must be a handgun. There is no listing of types, caliber or manufacturer of the handgun. They do state that you cannot use your Concealed Carry License to carry a taser, stun gun, machine gun, short barreled rifle or short barreled shotgun, pneumatic gun, spring gun, pellet

gun, BB gun or paint ball gun.

"The application process is generally an online based
application, are there public computers which can be used
to input the data?"
The state mentions it is acceptable to use public library
computers to make the application.

The updated Illinois application system can also be
accessed and successfully inputted via smartphones and
tablets. If you do not have computer access, you can
contact the State Police Licensing Unit and obtain a paper
copy of the application or they may take and input your
information over the telephone via (217) 782-7980 at the
ISP Firearms Services Customer Service Center.

"Can out of state residents obtain an Illinois License to
Carry?"
Only if they are subject to "similar" firearms laws in their
own state Only Hawaii, South Carolina and Virginia have
been found to be enough similar that Illinois would allow
application from residents of those states.
https://cc14illinois.com/ccw/Public/Faq.aspx

"Will other states recognize the Illinois Concealed Carry
License?"
The state of Illinois website does not list other states which
may recognize the Illinois permit and states it is the
responsibility of the license holder to research the matter in
any other state in which they wish to carry a handgun.
There are a number of online websites and cell phone apps

which have up to date information on reciprocity by other states and the actual text of those state laws.

"The basic course of instruction is a 16 hour program, but some parties only have to complete an 8 hour program. Who is eligible for the 8 hour waiver?"

Active duty, retired and honorably discharged military veterans only have to complete an 8 hour course. They are given credit for their military firearms training.

"Are Department of Natural Resources Hunter Safety Courses eligible for credit as part of the training process?"
The Concealed Carry Instructor can grant up to 4 hours of credit for successful completion of an Illinois Hunter Safety Course.

"Does a state resident have to register a firearm sale with the state when selling to a private party?"
Both parties have always had to have an FOID card and keep a record of the sale/purchase for 10 years. However, as of 2014, under 430 ILCS 65/3 (a-10), the seller MUST contact the State Police with the purchaser's FOID number and date of birth to insure the FOID is valid prior to sale of a firearm, stun gun or taser. The ISP will provide the seller an approval number valid for 30 days which should be listed on the sales paperwork. Call (217) 782-7980 at the ISP Firearms Services Customer Service Center or enter the FOID information online on the ISP website.
https://www.ispfsb.com/Public/Firearms/FOID/PersonToPe rsonFirearmTransfer.aspx

CHAPTER THREE
THE FOUR RULES OF FIREARMS SAFETY.

The Illinois state application process requires a specific training curriculum for Concealed Carry License, and must cover all shooters and gun owners from beginner to expert. Safety is obviously the center of all firearms training.

The following four safety rules cannot be overstated or repeated often enough. The safety rules never stop applying even with years of practice-and actually become more critical over time if familiarity breeds a lack of caution. Firearm "accidents" are absolutely preventable.

Violation of any of the following rules can endanger your life or the lives of others.

1. TREAT EVERY GUN AS IF IT WERE LOADED
2. KEEP YOUR FINGER OFF THE TRIGGER UNTIL READY TO FIRE
3. DO NOT POINT A GUN AT ANYTHING YOU ARE NOT WILLING TO SHOOT OR DESTROY
4. BE AWARE OF YOUR BACKSTOP AND BEYOND

Treat every gun as if it were loaded

Always. Every day. Every night. From Magnum to BB gun, and especially if you think it is unloaded. People get shot by accident with "unloaded guns" because they fail to follow this rule. If you pick up a gun, check inside to see if it is in fact loaded or unloaded. Never hand a gun over to another person without insuring to yourself it is unloaded. Never accept a gun at face value or the phrase "Don't worry, it's not loaded."

To insure a gun is safe, the action must be opened and visually inspected and then physically inspected by carefully placing a finger into the chamber area to insure nothing resides there. To be absolutely sure, look away and then look back and inspect it again. Hand over any weapon with the breach open or revolver cylinder out of the frame. This is safe for both parties. If you are not familiar with the action say so or do not touch the gun.

Even BB guns, pellet guns and blank firing guns should be treated as if they were loaded at all times and dangerous. Despite the fact they are "less gun" they can still injure someone if they are loaded and discharge.

Keep your finger off the trigger until ready to fire.

Safe gun handling requires you never put your finger on the trigger unless you are aimed in on target and ready to fire. Moving while holding a loaded weapon may be done safely if the owner's finger is not on the trigger. Most pistols have internal safeties which prevent accidental discharges or mechanical failures resulting in accidental discharges. Some have external safeties as well, but no safety can take the place of keeping the trigger finger or other obstructions off of the trigger and out of the trigger guard. Most trained gun handlers lay their trigger finger alongside the pistol frame. The trigger finger can move onto the trigger in a fraction of a second if need be, but it is absolutely safe alongside the frame and the gun may be carried or moved about without danger of accidental discharge.

Each shooter must train themselves to keep their finger off the trigger. It is not a natural thing, and must be learned and repeated so it becomes muscle memory as well as a conscious decision to treat each weapon as if it were always loaded.

Never point a gun at anything you are not willing to shoot or destroy.

Always keep your gun pointed in a safe direction. Pretend there is a powerful laser beam burning from the barrel of your weapon at all times. If you sweep the muzzle of the gun around a room the laser would destroy everything it touches-just like a bullet would if it were discharged. Do not sweep your muzzle across people or anything you are not willing to destroy.

Outdoors, down is usually a safe direction to point your gun. Dirt is good. Pointing it up in the air is not always a good idea or safe depending on overhead power sources, structures or even aircraft. A bullet exits the muzzle at a high rate of speed and may travel hundreds of yards unless it strikes an obstacle. Even the tiny and popular .22 long rifle cartridge has a warning on the box stating the bullet may travel up to one mile.

Some trainers talk of having a "safety circle", a six inch circle on the ground a foot or so in front of the shooter or gun handler. Keeping the muzzle pointed down in

14

the circle while standing still or moving insures it is pointed in a safe direction.

Indoors, a safe direction to point the muzzle of a gun may be difficult to find. There may be people who are living above you or beside you or below you. Look for an area that contains a hard surface away from living spaces. Residence walls are not considered to be hard surfaces. Most modern pistol bullets have the ability to penetrate several layers of drywall or wall material.

Be aware of your backstop and beyond

This insures you are not only looking at a target, but have some reason to believe the backstop behind the target will stop the round, control any missed rounds or prevent ricochets. If you are in a self-defense situation, being aware of the areas behind a threat may make a big impact on how to proceed. Are there other people behind the walls? You certainly don't want to endanger your family or innocent bystanders.

CHAPTER FOUR
PLACES IN ILLINOIS YOU CANNOT CARRY A CONCEALED WEAPON-EVEN IF YOU HAVE A LICENSE

As stated elsewhere, Illinois is the last state in the nation to codify and enact the right to Concealed Carry. The fear mongers always touted blood would be running in the streets if more citizens had guns. This of course is contrary to the actual facts proven up in all of the 49 other states. When law abiding citizens have more guns, they are safer and there is less crime. There are no gunfights in the streets or vigilante justice taking place and violent crime rates go down.

Illinois lawmakers provided a long list of locations where you cannot carry a concealed weapon even if you have a Concealed Carry License and private businesses are mandated to post Gun Free Zone signs.

The Gun Free Zone is denoted via a very visible square 4" X 6" white sign with a black pistol on it with a cross out red circle on it.

PROHIBITED LOCATIONS
430 Illinois Compiled Statute Sections 66/65(a).

A. Schools-All buildings, grounds and parking areas associated with either private or public schools are off limits to those legally carrying weapons.

B. Child care and preschools are also off limits. This includes the buildings, the property and parking lots associated with the caretaking and education of young children not enrolled in K-12 grades. Persons who operate daycare in their home can still own and possess weapons in the home, but they must be stored in a locked container when a child who is being care taken is present in the home.

C. Government buildings associated with the legislative or executive branch. This includes the buildings themselves, the grounds and parking lots. There is a note in this section that advises the Department of Natural Resources may enact laws in public hunting areas controlled by the Wildlife Code (example: You cannot carry a firearm while engaged in archery deer season)

D. The State Supreme Court, Appellate Courts and Circuit Courts buildings, grounds and parking areas. Any building that is used as a public court or any building where even a portion of the building is used for public court is off limits for Concealed Carry.

E. Local government buildings are also off limits like city halls, town halls or village buildings.

F. Prisons and jails and any facility that is used as an adult or juvenile detention or correctional facility. This includes the building, grounds and parking facilities.

G. Hospitals, mental health facilities and nursing homes. This includes buildings, grounds and parking areas owned or controlled by public or private hospitals, mental health facilities or nursing homes.

H. Buses, trains or other public forms of transportation. The reason this law applies to these forms of transportation, is there are public taxes and funds which help support them and thus the state government can prohibit Concealed Carry on those conveyances, in buildings, grounds and parking areas connected with those transport entities like city bus stations, train stations, subways and elevated train stations and platforms.

I. Bars, restaurants or establishments which serve alcohol on the premises. Again this covers the building, grounds and parking lots. In a rare twist, the law puts a measure of responsibility upon the owners of those businesses to post signs announcing no firearms are allowed. The statute states the establishment is off-limits if more than 50% of the business's gross receipts within the prior three months are from the sale of alcohol. The Concealed Carry License Holder will have no idea of the percentage of alcohol sales a restaurant contributes and the burden is on the business. If they fail to follow the law, or make false statements about the percentage of gross receipts, this can subject the business to prosecution under the state Liquor Control Act.

J. Public gatherings or special events which require licenses and are conducted on public property like parades or festivals. The law does not prevent a License a Concealed Carry Holder who has to walk through the area to get to their home, vehicle or place of business.

K. Special events or special use licenses under the state liquor control act-buildings and property with Special Event Retailer's license under the Liquor Control Act.

L. Public play grounds. Any and all public playgrounds are off limits to firearms.

M. Public parks, publicly owned or managed athletic areas associated with municipalities or park districts. The statute states is not designed to prohibit a Concealed Carry License holder from carrying a legally concealed pistol while on a trail or bicycle path where only a portion of the trail or bikeway includes a public park.

N. The entire Cook County Forest Preserve District and all associated properties and parking areas are off limits.

O. Colleges and Universities-public and private institutions to include buildings, classrooms, laboratories, clinics, hospitals, artistic venues, athletic venues, entertainment venues, college related properties (owned and leased) and grounds, parking areas, common areas, sidewalks and areas under the control of any public or private community college, college or university.

P. Gambling facilities to include buildings, properties or parking areas of businesses subject to the Illinois State Riverboat Gambling Act or the Horse Racing Act of 1975 and off track or inter track waging locations.

Q. Stadiums, arenas, college or professional sporting events. This includes the buildings, arenas, grounds and parking areas at any professional or college level sporting events.

R. Libraries-any building, property or parking area owned or under the control of a library. The statute does not list private libraries as being separate from public libraries.

S. Airports to include buildings, grounds and parking areas. If you are travelling with a firearm via an airline, you must declare it to the air carrier and secure it in a locking container while unloaded in checked baggage. It is very important to know an

Illinois Concealed Carry License does not allow anyone to transit an Illinois airport, through security or to board an airplane while armed.

T. Amusement parks are also areas prohibited from concealed carry. All buildings, property and parking areas are off limits to concealed carry.

U. Zoos and museums, their buildings, property and parking limits are areas prohibited from concealed carry.

V. Nuclear Energy, storage, weapons or development sites or facilities. License holders cannot store a firearm or ammunition in their vehicle or in a container in a vehicle even unloaded and secured on any property associated with nuclear facilities.

W. Any area where firearms are prohibited under federal law. Examples would include aircraft, Social Security facilities, Post Offices, Federal Courthouses, and military bases.

X. Posted areas. The owner of any private property or business may self-prohibit the carrying of otherwise legally concealed firearms on their property-even when a valid Concealed Carry License is present. According to the Illinois law, the owner must post a 4 in x 6 in sign-unless the property is a private residence. The Concealed Carry License law is never meant to trample the rights of property owners or business operators. Businesses have the right to refuse entry of concealed weapons. To be fair and prevent problems, they must post the no firearms notice in a prominent location.

IMPORTANT PARKING LOT EXEMPTIONS-What if I arrive with my weapon and find out it is not allowed on the property or inside buildings?

Under the state law, 430 ILCS 66/65(b), if a Concealed Carry License holder arrives and finds they are not allowed to proceed further into an institution, building, ground or parking area they "shall be licensed to carry a concealed firearm on or about his person within a vehicle into the parking areas, and may store a firearm or ammunitions concealed in a case within a locked vehicle or locked container out of plain view within the vehicle in the parking area." A License holder who discovers a building or grounds are off limits may carry their legally concealed firearm to their vehicle within even a prohibited parking area for the limited purpose of storing or retrieving a firearm in the trunk if the License holder ensures the firearm is unloaded prior to exiting the vehicle.

The law defines the case or container to include glove box or console compartment which completely encloses the concealed firearm or ammunition, the trunk or a firearm carrying box, shipping box or other container.

Attempts to merely place the weapon under a seat do not meet the definition of a container. It is a foolish and dangerous choice which may lead to theft or law enforcement interaction, and is a serious safety issue since anyone who transits or rides in the vehicle may access it.

CARRYING CONCEALED WHILE HUNTING

Since the Illinois law cites the conservation and hunting authorities can impose rules which impact on the right to carry concealed weapons some quotes from the Illinois Department of Natural Resources (IDNR) web sites Frequently Asked Questions are included below:

"CONCEALED CARRY LICENSE QUESTIONS & ANSWERS RELATED TO HUNTING IN ILLINOIS

"May a person possessing a valid Illinois Concealed Carry License carry a concealed firearm when deer or turkey hunting?

Under the current regulations, Concealed Carry License holders are not allowed to possess any firearm, including a concealed firearm, when deer or turkey hunting unless the firearm carried is legal for taking the species being hunted. For example, an archery deer hunter would not be able to carry any firearm, whether concealed or not, when archery deer hunting. However, if a concealed carry License holder is hunting deer during the legal "firearm" deer seasons, he/she may carry a concealed firearm, but only if that firearm is of the legal type for firearm deer hunting.

http://www.dnr.illinois.gov/hunt/Pages/HuntingTrappingDigests.aspx.

(2) May an Illinois Concealed Carry License holder, who is training or running hunting dogs during the period when the hunting season is closed, carry a concealed firearm? No, unless such firearm is a pistol capable of firing only blank cartridges. In addition, no person in the dog training party shall be in possession of live ammunition.

(3) May an Illinois Concealed Carry License holder be in possession of a concealed firearm when hunting any species, with the exception of questions 1 and 2 above? Yes. With the exception of deer, turkey, or dog training as explained in questions 1 and 2 above, an Illinois Concealed Carry License holder may possess a concealed firearm on their person or in their motor vehicle while in the field hunting any species of wildlife, unless the Concealed Carry License holder is in one of the prohibited areas listed in the Illinois Concealed Carry Act.

(4) May an Illinois Concealed Carry License holder use his/her concealed firearm to shoot the species which they are hunting?

Only if the concealed firearm carried is authorized by the Wildlife Code to take (shoot) the particular species of wildlife being hunted.

(5) On what IDNR properties may an Illinois Concealed Carry License holder carry a concealed firearm?

24

Illinois Concealed Carry License holders may carry a concealed firearm on any IDNR real property (including bike trails, trails, or any other designated public hunting area or building where firearm possession is Licensed by the IDNR) with the following exceptions: All IDNR Office buildings, including but not limited to the Joel D. Brunsvold Building (IDNR Springfield Headquarters Building), IDNR Regional Office buildings, IDNR State Museum buildings, and any other IDNR building marked with the ISP-approved sign prohibiting firearms. All firearms, including concealed firearms, are also prohibited on all IDNR State Refuge areas, IDNR Dedicated Nature Preserves, and IDNR children playground areas.

(6) Can an Illinois Concealed Carry License holder possess a concealed firearm on or in a watercraft, off-highway vehicle, or snowmobile?

Yes, but only if the watercraft, off-highway vehicle, or snowmobile is operated in an area not prohibited under the Concealed Carry Act."

CHAPTER FIVE
THE ILLINOIS DEFINITIONS OF JUSTIFIABLE USE OF FORCE.

 Many people have been told things third hand or claim to "know the law" when it comes to firearms and deadly force, but there is no substitute for the actual law the state uses to evaluate and judge whether a citizen is justified in their use of force.

This is a reality check. Gun owners must know the law and cannot delude themselves violent situations will all be resolved in a positive manner just because they have a legally concealed firearm on their person. A life and death encounter is different than watching it on television-the repercussions will continue for the rest of your life, and may include incarceration and/or law suits.

There is a famous phrase that is appropriate here "Every bullet has a lawyer attached to it".

Those who review a post-shooting situation will have months or years to gather more information or study a decision which was made in mere seconds. A gun owner must understand the law and honestly evaluate their choices knowing they must survive intense scrutiny.

There is a mantra passed down from the Shaolin monks who first practiced Kung Fu: "Avoid rather than Check. Check rather than Block. Block rather than Strike. Strike rather than Kill." Avoiding the situation is almost always the best solution. Even though you may have a legal right to carry a gun and have training and experience, it is always better to avoid a confrontation than to escalate the situation. Remember it will always be seen by critics later as a gun fight-and you brought a gun to the incident.

Avoiding the use of your legally concealed firearm or even a retreat does not seem like a John Wayne situation-but John Wayne was a movie actor. Bravery is not in question here. Self-preservation so you can go home to your loved ones and enjoy another day trumps all other considerations short of life and death necessity.

In an emergency, or armed conflict situation, move to cover or out of the area, maintain your vigilance and contact 911 if necessary. Protect yourself and your family by avoiding problems in the first place or in the moment maneuver them out of harm's way with your oversight and protection. Freshly minted gun carriers and martial artists often look for fights. The more experienced fighters instead look for opportunities to avoid the confrontations and get better at spotting potentially dangerous situations far ahead of time.

 The yardstick to court or prosecutor reviews of deadly force encounters in American jurisprudence has most frequently been evaluated in the court system as "reasonableness". The situation should be judged by the law, police, prosecutors, judges and juries based upon the idea "What would a reasonable person do in this situation?" and "Were their actions reasonable after balancing all of the information available and acting upon it?" or "Was the amount of force used reasonable?"

We all believe we are reasonable people, and make reasonable decisions, (court houses and jails are full of people who were mistaken in this belief). With deadly force as an option, we cannot delude ourselves using TV knowledge or firearms myths as our guide. All firearm decisions must be fact based and made according to the standards required by law.

Use of Force In Defense of Persons.

Illinois lists the use of force in defense of persons under state law 720 ILCS 5/7-1. The Illinois law related to self-defense uses the "reasonableness" standard twice in the text of the actual law in subsection (a). Justifiable force is described below as the amount reasonably believed necessary to defend oneself or another against the imminent use of unlawful force, and deadly force (capable of causing death or great bodily harm) is only justified if you reasonably believe it is necessary to prevent imminent death or great bodily harm to oneself or others, or in the commission of a forcible (Violent) felony.

Subsection (b) advises if a person is found to have used justified reasonable force under this law against an aggressor they will not be subject to law suit or claim by the aggressor or their families.

This sounds like quite exoneration, and the way we would all like to be treated by our society. However, many weeks or months down the road if your actions are not found to have been reasonable in the matter of self-defense in the court system- you are not protected under this statute from further claims or suits. Again, it is always advisable to avoid a deadly force situation if at all possible.

"720 ILCS 5/7-1 Use of Force in Defense of Person

(a) "A person is justified in the use of force against another when and to the extent that he reasonably believes that such conduct is necessary to defend himself or another against such other's imminent use of unlawful force. However, he is justified in the use of force which is intended or likely to cause death or great bodily harm only if he reasonably believes that such force is necessary to prevent imminent death or great bodily harm to himself or another, or the commission of a forcible felony.

(b) In no case shall any act involving the use of force justified under this Section give rise to any claim or liability brought by or on behalf of any person acting within the definition of "aggressor" set forth in section (a) of this Article, or the estate, spouse, or other family member of such a person against the person or estate of the person using such justified force unless the use of force involves willful or wanton misconduct."

(Source: P.A. 93-832, eff 7-28-04)

Use of Force In a Dwelling.

Illinois also has a statute related to the use of force in defense of a dwelling or residence under 720 ILCS 5/7-2. The old common law belief that "a man's home is his castle" has received considerable protection in the United States and codified in the 4th Amendment to the

Constitution to prevent the government conducting illegal searches and seizures in our homes. Next to the contents of the human body, our homes have received the most protections at law by the U.S. law makers and U.S. court systems.

But you cannot shoot people just to prevent trespass or to protect property. Deadly force can only be an option to prevent death or serious injury to persons not property. Under the Illinois law (below), the defender must reasonably believe they need to use force to prevent or stop unlawful entry/attack into the dwelling; but only if, (1) the entry is made in a violent fashion and the defender reasonably believes the use of force is necessary to prevent assault upon themselves or another, or (2) the defender reasonably believes such force is necessary to prevent the commission of a felony in the dwelling.

Many people keep firearms in their homes to protect themselves and their families (the FBI estimates personal possession at over 200 million guns). It should never be claimed they are keeping those guns just to protect personal property. They are being kept by law abiding citizens to protect their lives and the lives of others.

 Many people also believe they should respond aggressively to any entry into their home and are justified in whatever force they need to defend their "castle." At law all of the elements to protect human life must be present to justify the use of force. Not all use of force is reasonable, and if there is no violent entry or no danger to humans, other options must be followed.

There is no way to tell what is in the head or heart of a burglar or trespasser. There is no easy way to ascertain their true intent, criminal history, mental state or level of intoxication. How can you know how violent they may be?

Luckily, we are not held to an impossible standard of care for those people. The statute lays out the entry must be violent and the use of force is necessary to prevent or stop the entry which is intended or likely to cause death or great bodily harm or a felony against the occupants. The homeowner or resident is allowed to use their individual judgment and no two persons face these situations with the same level of training or abilities. How you perceive the threat and are able to describe it will also be critical in the aftermath.

There are myths related to "If you shoot burglars outside your house just drag them inside and you are covered under the law". This is not a true statement of the law, and tampering with a shooting scene or lying to police are both criminal offenses. If all of the required elements for the use of force in a dwelling are present it should not matter where a shooting victim falls.

Similar to subsection (b) for self-defense use of force, the use of force statute for defense of dwelling has a subsection (b) which relates if all of the elements for use of force are met under the law in subsection (a) no aggressor or their family will be allowed to bring suit against the defender who used justified force.

Another self-defense issue/castle idea should be addressed here. The idea you should get a gun and go confront someone breaking in to your dwelling- is not always tactically sound.

It certainly appeals at an emotional level, but depending on location and circumstances, would it be safer to contact 911 for help, collect your family and barricade in a room with a firearm, phone and flashlight instead of moving around inside a darkened house making noise and risking a deadly force encounter with unknown intruder(s)?

Safety rule #4 "Be aware of your backstops and beyond" certainly applies in dwellings. Pistols, shotguns and rifles will all easily penetrate multiple thicknesses of drywall and plywood used in the construction of homes. They may also travel into neighboring houses. If you have to shoot, shoot to stop the aggression, but shoot accurately and know any misses run the risk of wall penetration.

"(720 ILCS 5/7-2)(from Ch. 38, par 7-2) Sec 7-2. Use of force in defense of dwelling.

(a) A person is justified in the use of force against another when and to the extent that he reasonably believes that such conduct is necessary to prevent or terminate such other's unlawful entry into or attack upon a dwelling. However he is justified in the use of force which is intended or likely to cause death or great bodily harm only if:

(1) The entry is made or attempted in a violent, riotous, or tumultuous manner, and he reasonably believes that such force is necessary to prevent an assault upon or offer of personal

violence to him or another then in the dwelling, or

(2) He reasonably believes that such force is necessary to prevent the commission of a felony in the building.

(b) In no case shall any act involving the use of force justified under this Section give rise to any claim or liability brought by or on behalf of any person acting within the definition of "aggressor" set forth in Section 7-4 of this Article, or the estate, spouse, or other family member of such a person, against the person or estate of the person using such justified force, unless the use of force involves willful or wanton misconduct.
(Source: P.A. 93-832, eff. 7-28-04)"

Use of Force in a non-dwelling or away from home.

Illinois also has a statue for the use of force involving other property that is not a dwelling under 720 ILCS 5/7-3. This statute is designed to cover situations of self-defense and property away from the home.

The use of force must still be found to be <u>reasonable</u> and there can be no justified use of deadly force without the involvement of actions which are intended or likely to cause death or great bodily harm

This statute, like the others, requires the person using force to reasonably believe they have to use force to stop the trespass or other tortious or criminal interference on the real estate property or personally owned property of themselves, their family member or someone they have a duty to protect.

Deadly force is only allowed if they reasonably believe that amount of force is necessary to prevent the commission of a forcible felony. There is a subsection (b) clause which again prevents aggressors from bringing suit or claim against the defender if they are found to have acted reasonably under the law.

The term "real property" in the statute is a legal term which refers to land or real estate. Personal property consists of all other types of property which are owned by a person or business and is moveable and not affixed to the land.

"(720 ILCS 5/7-3) (From Ch. 38, par 7-3)

Sec. 7-3. Use of force in defense of other property.

    (a) A person is justified in the use of force against another when and to the extent that he reasonably believes that such conduct is necessary to terminate such other's trespass on or other tortious or criminal interference with either real property (other than a dwelling) or personal property lawfully in his possession or in the possession of another who is a member of their immediate family or household or of a person whose property he has a duty to protect. However, he is justified in the use of force which is intended or likely to cause death or great bodily harm only if he reasonably believes that such force is necessary to prevent the commission of a forcible felony.

(b) In no case shall any act involving the use of force justified under this section give rise to any claim or liability brought by or on behalf of any person acting within the definition of "aggressor" set forth in Sections (a) of this article, or the estate, spouse, or other family member of such a person or against the person or estate of the person using such justified force, unless the use of force involves willful or wanton misconduct.

(c) (Source: P.A. 93-832, eff. 7-28-04.)"

CHAPTER SIX
LIVING IN A HEIGHTENED STATE OF AWARENESS.

How do you avoid being in life or death situations and survive deadly force gunplay? Quite honestly, you should see the elements or red flags already present and potential danger as it develops-possibly before the bad guy initiates any overt action.

Most events do not happen spontaneously no matter how it appears to a witness who "suddenly" notices aggressive behavior. Criminals don't exist in a vacuum. They give off distinct warning signs. They behave and dress aggressively, and are usually quite noticeable to anyone who has the slightest tactical mindset. If you are also working within a critical time constraint, critical thinking and rapid decisions can help you more than having the best pistol ever invented on your hip.

Consider sharks here. Sharks are not inherently bad. They are just eating machines. It is in their nature. However, they exhibit very distinct and exaggerated body movements before they attack. They drop their dorsal fins, become quite rigid and exaggerated in their moments before attacking. Even without raising their voice, human beings frequently exhibit similar exaggerated behaviors prior to attack.

Speech may become loud, choppy or stilted. Shoulders are angled, hands come up to chest level and heads drop lower. Eye contact becomes fixed and rigid. These body language clues by people under the influence of alcohol or drugs are easier to identify because their brains are slowed down or addled, and they of course do not realize they are telegraphing their aggression.

It is also frequently announced by the oh-so iconic drunken phrase "I am gonna kick your ass!" Observe, make tactical decisions about it, and initiate an action plan before it happens. Don't wait for the attack. Intentions have already been announced.

There is a law enforcement phrase related to aggression "Only cops and crooks look you in the eye." Try it and see. In the wild or on the street, predators fixate on the eyes of victims. They are looking for weakness on one side and potential victims are looking for signs of aggression and attack on the other side. Notice the next time you are walking outdoors or in a store and some American makes eye contact with you-is it a street criminal or a nice old lady?

Learn to recognize direct eye contact as a challenge or a sign of potential aggression. With crooks, they are looking for challenges from other wild creatures and also looking for position of dominance over weaker creatures. Drive down your street and see how many people make eye contact with you. Drive down a bad street and notice how many people deliberately check you out with solid eye contact as you drive by. People who live in high crime areas watch other people with a much higher interest than you probably do in your day to day life.

Not all aggressive behavior is random, although it may seem like it if you have been day dreaming or not paying attention. Most attackers have pre-selected victims they think they can overcome with little to no risk to themselves. Using another nature analogy, in the wild, the king of predators were African lions, and lions do not hunt and feast on a diet of other lions. They eat sick, weak and slow animals that do not have big teeth and claws. They prefer to not attack animals who fight back, or who are aware of their predatory presence. They attack to dominate and win. The same principles apply to human predators.

Carry yourself in the moment, not distracted by cell phones and music. Carry yourself with head up and searching with your eyes for potential danger or ambushes. If you are not feeling well or are distracted (like most of us can be) you have to set it aside until you are in a safe area where you can let your guard down.

Colonel Jeff Cooper was an icon in developing "modern" gun fighting tactics. Colonel Cooper was also famous for thinking about and talking about living a life with guns. He coined some adages about training yourself to live in a heightened state of awareness. The concept is very simple "Pay more attention to the world around you!"

He is credited with coming up with color codes related to how attentive people should live their lives. If you are going to carry a gun or perhaps even more so if you don't have a gun, teach yourself to live in a heightened state of awareness as you float about your particular aquarium.

38

CONDITION WHITE-Paraphrased here, condition white applies to people who go about their daily lives fairly oblivious to their surroundings or conditions that may be hazardous to them. Most of our friends and neighbors live their lives in this manner. Other people have called them sheep, very non-violent, group animals that spend most of their lives with their heads down grazing.

Colonel Cooper did not live long enough to have to witness the cell phone phenomenon currently seen all across the world. Whenever we slow down or have a 20 second gap of entertainment or waiting in line, those cellphones pop out. People bury themselves inside those tiny screens and disengage from the real world around them.

Colonel Cooper was a pretty serious guy, and had he lived longer I am pretty sure he would have remarked upon the use of cellphones and ear bud music players currently being used to blank out the world around us.

CONDITION YELLOW- The next higher level of awareness in this series is condition yellow, a more active state than white. Think of condition yellow as being similar to defensive driving for the rest of your life, not just while driving.

TEACH YOURSELF TO LIVE IN CONDITION YELLOW WHEN YOU ARE OUT IN PUBLIC. This is actively looking for areas of possible problem or threat where ever you go. Watch stranger's eyes and hands on the street, listen for footsteps behind you-watch shadows, and watch for groups of young males at corners. In restaurants look at the patrons, select better vantage points where to sit, don't sit with your back to the door, look for multiple exits and pay attention to loud noises and loud people. In your car, when you pull up to a stop sign or light check the drivers and cars next to you. If someone parallels you while driving definitely check on their face and hands instead of just driving blindly on.

We shouldn't drive in bad neighborhoods at night, yet we all do it through bad planning or by accident on occasion. If you suddenly notice you have gone awry, then pay attention to the amount of graffiti in your area, amount of garbage and disrepair of property along the street, and people lounging or grouping at the corners.

 The more graffiti you see and more bars on windows and doors the more high risk the neighborhood you are in. Ratchet up your defenses. Insure your doors are locked and keep space cushions around your car in case you have to maneuver suddenly.

Condition yellow is not paranoia; it is just being more active living your life and paying attention to the world around you. No one can stay there all the time, you need to have time to relax, but that is a time when you are more secure like at home. When you are moving about in public do it with your head up and being at least slightly more alert than you were yesterday. Remind yourself when you find yourself drifting off or slipping back into condition white.

CONDITION ORANGE- This is the phase where you have identified an actual threat or impending problem. Start moving now. Don't wait until it gets worse. By being aware of your threat conditions you should be a half step ahead of bad guy behavior. Don't sort through too many options and devote long thoughts about being politically correct, just move!

If you have action plans in your head implement immediately. Move away, move to cover, put your hand on your gun, or start drawing your gun. Direct others as necessary-they will take direction in an emergency if you direct them. If left to stand and stare, they are just another potential victim. In a loud and clear voice tell them "Get down." " Go to the car." " Get behind cover." Do you have time to call 911? Probably not, but you can direct someone else, a non-gun handler to do so. "CALL 911. DO IT NOW!"

CONDITION RED- This is fight or flight time. Extraneous thinking and having to extrapolate on long term decisions won't be much good to you. You are working in a rapidly ticking time bubble and need to move- hopefully in a manner you have previously practiced and/or previously thought about. MOVE. Don't be a standing target. Move to get out of the target zone and/or move to cover. If you are deploying your gun you need to be moving. A moving target is much harder to hit.

CONDITION BLACK- This is the worst of all possible conditions. Condition black is panic. You are so overwhelmed by violence or fear of a threat you don't know what to do, or what to think. If you are befuddled trying to understand the situation or the motivation for the bad guy or don't wish to offend their sensibilities- you can't save yourself. You can't make plans, take cover and you are not moving. Trying to figure out the motivations of the crook during the actual event is just lost time or hoping they won't harm you is relying totally upon the kind and gentle nature of a criminal.

In Condition Black you are just a large, cash laden non-moving blood and organ filled target for whatever the bad guy chooses to deliver. In condition black the situation is only over when the bad guy decides it is over, because you can't make conscious survival choices or initiate violence of action or flight on your own. Even sudden running away and yelling for help is much better than saying nailed to the target X in Condition Black.

CHAPTER SEVEN
THINKING ABOUT WHEN TO DEPLOY YOUR GUN.

If you have decided to take the training and apply for a concealed carry license you have obviously thought about the commitment to having and carrying a firearm. You also need to spend some time thinking about what concealed carry means to you and set some boundaries about when you would engage in a deadly force encounter.

This may include very specific legal constraints imposed by the state, your own moral code, religious upbringing, life experience and sense of ethics. It is not all steely eyed quick draw fantasies. Concealed carry can be a definite positive in your life, but a number of burdens come with it. You need to have some of those issues and your local laws settled in your mind before going too much further.

Preplanning responses in conjunction with abilities and gun handling skills have great impact on what you can do in the event you are brought into a deadly force situation. If you have movement and decision options available and a certain skill handling firearms, it is more than likely you won't have to shoot-but could if you have to. You may be able to terminate or leave this situation without firing a shot. This is a huge option and much less likely to embroil you in extended court and media trials.

You will be involved in a lot more non-fights than real fights. It is easier on your nerves, your bank account, and far less paperwork. The problem with a potential gun fight is you brought the gun. You can't waffle on the use of your gun, either it is used correctly or not at all. In the eyes of the law you have to be right every time.

You may believe there are super-secret gun fighting tactics practiced by high speed military units that would make up for your lack of day to day gunfight experience. "Oh if only I could go to the schools they go to, then I would be awesome too." Well, most of advanced gun handling training includes manipulating the trigger correctly while the sights are aligned correctly and repeating it several thousand times.

With repetition, you get to increase speed and accuracy, but the actual tactics related to movement and deployment are more derived from the American police and competition shooters than from military training or combat situations. Understand this: no one in the military voluntarily goes into a shooting situation armed with only a pistol. They want a rifle and at least a squad of similarly armed riflemen with them.

If you already know how to pull a trigger well and align the sights and have the where-with-all to save your own life, then you need to have some practical application plans in your head in case the feces hits the oscillating device. The middle of a shoot on a dark and rainy night, is not a good place to learn or try to apply new "tactics."

If you are "learning" from watching YouTube videos challenge everything. YouTube is awash with "experts". Some things you see are good, some are ridiculous. Take the parts you can use in a legal and ethical matter, and dismiss the parts that don't work.

If you are not comfortable with your gun, you might think carrying it with the chamber empty is a "safer" way to carry it. Get that thinking out of your head. Treat Every Gun As If It Is Loaded all day every day, and carry it fully loaded and ready to fire in the shortest amount of time. In the heat of the moment you will have too many things to think about and stopping to charge the chamber with a live round is dangerous to you, costs additional time, and in the fray you may not remember to chamber a round, leaving you with a short stubby club when you really wanted a loaded gun.

Don't handicap yourself due to someone else's "tactics" or "combat training" and are you going to build in that empty chamber training scar-that you don't even trust yourself with a loaded gun?

If you are not confident carrying then how effective will you be if you decide you should draw down or start shooting at human beings?

As stated earlier, your actions must still be "reasonable" if you have to shoot at someone. It will also be just as important to be able to later verbalize to the police, or the courts, the fact you or someone else was in imminent danger of receiving a severe injury or death, before you engaged in a deadly force shooting scenario.

CRITICAL TEACHING POINT- POST SHOOTING VERBALIZATION OF THE FEAR YOU FELT AND THE DANGER PRESENT, WHICH MADE YOU SHOOT IN SELF DEFENSE, IS CRITICAL TO HOW YOU WILL BE VIEWED AND TREATED AFTER A SHOOTING AND WILL EFFECT THE REST OF YOUR LIFE.

GUNFIGHTING ZEN- QUOTE OF THE DAY.
"If someone has a gun and is trying to kill you, it would be reasonable to shoot back with your own gun" – Dalai Lama May 15, 2001.

RED FLAGS FOR ENGAGEMENT WITH A FIREARM.
Having some red flag items already in your mental filing cabinet will allow faster recognition of a developing deadly encounter. Keep an open list going in your head that includes "Gun!", "Knife!", "Club!", "Verbal Threats!", "No Exits!", "Multiple Bad Guys!", "Family at Risk!" and add other items to match your personal abilities or personal problem areas to be able to defend against or avoid.

Being placed in fear of receiving a great bodily harm. In the history of self-defense down through the ages, the immortal drug addled, violent or drunken threats, like "I am going to kill you" or "I am going to kick your ass!" can place you in fear of receiving a great bodily harm. Or not.

Everyone is different. If the jerk of the moment does not seem to have the ability to carry out the threat, then obviously you are not in fear of receiving a bodily harm and most likely should not shoot them for their lack of manners!

If you feel that you are indeed threatened by this person, in the manner they are announcing and they seem to have the ability to carry it out, then their threat goes to the top of the list and it is time to bring deadly force options to the table..

If you are small, then "Much Bigger Attacker" gets added to the list. If you are alone, then "Multiple Attackers" gets on the list. If you can't physically move, retreat, run or walk to avoid younger or more nimble attackers, then those factors go on the list as well.

If I you enough GO and NO GO plans in that giant filing cabinet in your head, you may understand developing situations or see red flags further down the road than someone else would. Get moving ahead of time sooner than just standing there flat footed watching it happen.

No-go. Don't shoot.
You should have some "NO GO" items on your list of Don't Shoot scenarios.

Not feeling you are in real fear of receiving a great bodily injury is a NO GO. If you just don't believe the threat is real you can't shoot.

Using a gun to protect only property is a NO GO (You can only protect human life with deadly force.) The presence of innocent bystanders in the target area should be on the NO GO list (remember the big four Safety Rules- Be aware of your back stops and beyond and never point your gun at anything you are not willing to shoot or destroy).

Shooting at moving vehicles with a pistol is also probably a NO GO. Chances of disabling the vehicle with a pistol are pretty much zero. If you do hit the driver of a moving vehicle, where will the car end up-did you just create a high speed 3,000 lb unguided missile?

Shooting at tires or radiators with a pistol won't stop a car in your life time, and hitting a driver through the glass is difficult to do when the car is just standing still. Adding movement and curved laminated windshield glass makes it exponentially tougher to shoot inside vehicles as well.

If they are going to kill you with a car, would you be better off spending scant seconds amount of time moving out of the way, versus standing and shooting at the oncoming car knowing it will take you a couple of seconds to deploy your gun and hit a stationary target...and knowing it won't stop the car?

Alcohol is a NO GO. Bringing your gun to a shooting situation after you have been drinking is a definite NO GO. This should go without saying but drinking and guns is a poor combination, and in a post shooting situation the presence of alcohol will be seen as reckless or brings extra scrutiny/criticism to your actions. On the practical side you won't be making clear decisions, your reaction time will be slowed, and you will be boiled alive by fiendish liability lawyers in the aftermath.

In a house, are you going to risk shooting towards the rooms housing children/family that are protected behind mere drywall or hollow core doors when your pistol bullet can penetrate several rooms worth of drywall? NO GO. (Be aware of your back stop and beyond!)

Are you going to shoot long distances with your pistol? Can you shoot and hit human sized targets at 50 yards? If not, then that is a NO GO. If you can do it, and practice at that distance, then you have more options. If you can't, then movement towards safety or cover may be your first/best choice. Stay within your competent/effective distances. If you are carrying a small gun with a short barrel, tiny grips and tiny sights you may be restricted to short self-defense distances. It is not just a noise maker-it contains the means for deadly force.

Warning shots are a NO GO. They are tactically unsound. Here are a few reasons why not to shoot a warning shot: You give away a free bullet that may be handy later in life. You give away a tactical advantage of surprise. Your gun could jam after that single bullet is fired. Other people will say you were the aggressor and the one who fired first. That bullet has to come down somewhere.

COVER VS CONCEALMENT

Your first priority to increase your odds of surviving a gunfight is to MOVE! Almost any movement will be an improvement as opposed to standing still, and moving to cover should be a priority. Get your feet moving towards cover.

We use cover to defeat incoming bullets if necessary. Anything that won't do that is not real cover. Skin and organs are notoriously poor at defeating bullets.

We need to put in our heads some idea of what "real" cover is. Most surfaces and items we encounter on a day to day basis are not really cover-they don't reliably stop bullets. If it doesn't stop bullets, then you are merely behind "concealment."

Concealment, is good to hide your shape and favorite organs, if that is all you have available in the moment. What you really want however, is good cover which can conceal you and protect you from in coming bullets and fragments. If you think for a moment or two about where you live, work and travel, most items around you are just concealment and not real cover.

Real cover, should be 100% effective at stopping bullets like-concrete, brick, two to four feet of dirt, rock, some metal (not all) and large trees. Everything else is just concealment. Even the ever present automobile, which seems like real cover, should be viewed as just concealment against pistol bullets. Pistol ammo can penetrate and exit most areas of a car except the engine block and rubber tires.

Rifles will make Swiss Cheese out of vehicles and bleeding passengers.

We have cars all around us, and you might duck to one for best cover in the moment. Just don't believe you are going to be completely safe unless you can get behind the wheels or engine area. (..and then don't stick your head up over the hood of the car!)

Well how about your house? Shouldn't that be good cover? Consider modern building materials. Drywall used to create walls is essentially just long sheets of chalk. Wooden doors may just be two thin veneers of light weight wood. You may be able to hide well in a house, but most of its contents short of refrigerators and stoves or other appliances are bullet penetrable.

This is not TV or the movies. How many times have you seen actors hiding behind sofas or coffee tables soaking up bullets? Those items in real life just hide your shape and probably leave you nursing bullet wounds with splinters in them.

In our present day, 5.56 ammo for the AR-15 is widely available on the street with a tungsten steel core penetrator in the bullet. It is government stock number M855 ammo and has a painted green tip to show it has the tungsten steel core. Otherwise it looks like any other ammo. It has been regaled as armor piercing ammo in the press. It is not true armor piercing, but it will absolutely poke holes in many things to include pistol rated vests and handsome and virile people inside them. This ammo was designed to shoot through Communists wearing body armor in a combat zone, and is widely available in the civilian commercial markets. It is not an ideal choice for shooting unarmored people due to a tendency to penetrate without expansion and just leaving small holes and small wounds.

AK-47's and SKS rifles have similar variant ammunition with a steel core. It is some of the cheapest rifle ammunition on the market. It will shoot through a telephone pole.

In a shooting situation, move to cover/concealment with the goal of getting to real cover if none is readily available. Movement with a draw of your gun to concealment is far better than standing still dueling it out with your pistol. Engaging from cover is much better than standing out in the open and you will feel good about your decisions later...because you will still be here!

If you have the time, watch this video on YouTube of a retail store clerk on the phone desperately wanting to get some cover by the end of the cash register counter and engaging with robbers in a shootout. "Excuse me. I'd like some cover please." Corn chips and beef jerky are not very good at being incoming projectile resistant.
https://www.youtube.com/watch?v=JUWX-4lRFjM

SHOOTING FROM COVER
Don't expose more of your body around cover than you are willing to get shot!

It used to be called barricade shooting, and people were taught to hide behind cover barricades and lean out to shoot at targets. Barricade shooting profiles on a gun range usually run the gamut from "Fairly Awful" to "Are you kidding me?" Most shooters just don't make use of the available cover in the belief "In a real gunfight I would do better." Use your available practice to make good decisions and repetitions. Bad practice is as bad as no practice. We fight like we train. (Ok, ok you knew that cliché was coming...good to get it out of the way.)

Most shooters expose an inordinate amount of their head and half of their body while shooting around barricades or even just stand next to the barricade during range practice.

Don't ground or brace your gun frame onto the barricade frame to make it a more stable shooting platform. Not all barricade material is solid enough to do this.

You an brace the backs of hands or knuckles on the barricade for stability, but this is also negated by less stable building materials. Current teaching protocols generally tell people to just shoot with your gun next to the barricade-don't touch it or lean on it. Also, you should not extend your gun barrel forward of the barricade like a door frame or window frame. This exposes more gun, more flesh, and someone you can't see around the corner could snatch your gun while crouched next to the barrier.

Many bad things can happen if you lean into a corner or barricade with the surface of your gun while you are attempting to make your gun more stable by leaning on that hard surface. (1) Movement in the materials will throw off your shot. (2) If you ground the barrel of your gun against a corner, it will also throw off the flight of your bullet. The natural vibration that results of the bullet passing through the barrel is interrupted or damped by touching a hard surface. (3) Pressing the slide of your semi-automatic against a hard surface will prevent it from being able to cycle correctly and can jam your gun after the first shot— about the time you really need to be able to make more shots! (4) With even ever dependable revolvers, you can prevent the cylinder from rotating if it is pressed against a hard surface-yes you can jam a revolver!

TEACH YOURSELF: Use doorways and corners in your house to assume a barricade shooting position. Look into a mirror on the other end of the room, or have someone video or take a picture of you or use a camera timer. You will see for yourself. Do you stick your whole head past the door frame? How about your leg/foot? Line up on the amount of cover you have then bend at the waist to lean over to the edge. Expose only your gun barrel and one eye if possible.

Try this on both right hand, and left hand door frames or corners. It might seem awkward on your weak hand side and you want to lean out further to extend your hands, your gun and both eyes. Can you instead just put your gun in your weak hand only and lean over exposing only your weak side eye? Of course you can. You probably just have never practiced this before. It is a far better use of cover than leaning all the way over with both hands extended and your brain box exposed.

RICOCHETS AND COVER

Keep in mind most bullets will ricochet off hard surfaces if struck at a shallow angle and continue to fly within six inches of the hard surface for a considerable distance. Now visualize trying to sneak down the hallway of a school or office building with cinder block or brick walls.

Inbound bullets will ricochet off those hard walls and can injure you. Moving through buildings you may have a natural tendency to hug or rub up against the walls in a hallway. Don't do it- stay a few inches off of those walls to avoid ricochet injuries. Another reason to stay off the walls-even though it seems to feel safer is sliding along those walls makes an inordinate amount of noise observable to people on the other side of those walls or down the hallway.

If you are stuck in a wide open hallway, move to your next form of cover/concealment quickly, generally the next doorway or piece of furniture. Sometimes you just have to suck it up and go, and substitute speed of movement to obtain some cover, versus your super-ninja stealth duck walk. It is a very lonely feeling walking up a long hallway with no cover and someone hiding or having cover at the other end. You feel like the world's biggest target. Don't linger in the open, and a lower profile is better than a tall profile.

If you are hiding behind the front wheel and engine block of a vehicle and stick your head up bad guy bullets can still skip off the flat hood and ricochet into your hard-to-miss pumpkin sized head. Try to stay at least 3 feet back from the vehicle you are using for cover so any ricochet rounds have a path that should open the angle and pass over the minimal part of your head seen above the hood.

Can you use these same ricochets and rules about hard cover against bad guys? Absolutely. You can skip rounds under cars or along walls. Even if you miss the bad guy but skip one across the hood into him it still counts! Can you shoot through cars, doors and walls? Yes you can. You are not guaranteed success and rounds may be deflected, but it is still a technique you can use. Someone once wrote that hiding behind cars as cover for you is "iffy", but you should not hesitate to shoot at bad guys who are using such iffy concealment themselves.

MORE ON THINKING ABOUT WHEN TO USE YOUR GUN.

Confront the myth of "I am a good shooter."

Studies of police shootings show the police actual hit percentages in the 10% and 20% range. Do they train more than you do? Maybe. Probably not. They do get very good training at the beginning of their career, and as techniques change they are introduced into their ongoing firearms training. But most likely they do not actually shoot as many bullets down range in a year as you do even if you are a casual shooter. Would you believe most police only shoot twice or four times a year? Would you also believe they shoot only 100 or 200 bullets in that year? Does that sound like what it takes to maintain being a "good shooter" to you? Are you that kind of "good"?

The other aspect which contributes to low hit percentages in police and civilian shootings is movement. The police don't train to shoot on the move much, and rarely get to shoot at moving targets.

Movement is an inherent part of gun fights or shootings. Shouldn't you train to anticipate it? Remember no one likes to be shot at. People are generally averse to getting shot at, and four out of five doctors recommend not getting killed when you have a choice.

People run, duck and weave like they are running for their life! It is nothing like standing on a range and banging away at a piece of paper. If you can, learn to shoot some reactive or moving targets, or move yourself around before or during firing.

If you are going to carry a gun for self-defense, you need to master that gun and holster system. You need to be able to consistently make center mass hits on close to medium ranges in a relatively quick amount of time. You need to be able to fix jams or misfeeds and conduct quick and efficient reloads-like one second reloads. No matter if you are civilian or police, shooting your gun two times a year is not going to leave you with enough residual training or muscle memory necessary to be "good".

"HOW LONG DO I HAVE TO RELOAD?"
ANSWER: "THE REST OF YOUR LIFE."

You need to practice. Yes it is expensive, and we have undergone some years of ammo shortages and price increases, but it is important to shoot and train if you plan on being able to use a gun to save your own life if called upon. You are worth it. Practice.

Shooting you did some years ago, does not really count for much today, unless it was training that instilled good muscle memory. If you choose to go without practice that is up to you, but when you do practice concentrate hard on the mechanics and don't go to "plink." How good you "used to be" does not equate into today or tomorrow if you don't keep honing that edge over time.

Your "muscle memory" degrades over time. An easy example that may make sense, is you also probably can't throw a baseball or football like you used to back in high school. If you think you can, you may be deluding yourself. We hope to rise to the occasion-but there should be some muscle memory or previous practice in place to fall back on.

OPEN CARRY VS CONCEALED CARRY TACTICS.

Quick tactics discussion on Open Carry vs Concealed Carry: A number of states allow "open carry" of pistols, ie. Guns worn openly, usually in holsters hanging on belts completely exposed to the public with no covering of any kind. What tactics are involved there? Are you extra vigilant? Are you distracted easily? Have you made yourself a guardian or a target?

There are nationwide movements afoot to get more state's to pass open carry laws as part of a bigger picture strategy to not only exercise 2nd amendment rights, but to enact legislation that guarantees more gun rights vs more restrictive views. However, if you can legally carry a concealed weapon in your state, why would you give away all tactical advantage and surprise in favor of openly carrying a pistol visible to the public? Open carry does cast a certain visible warning, but it also targets the carrier or paints them as a potential problem.

You also should exhibit even more vigilance as an open carrier than you do when carrying in concealed carry. You have to protect yourself and your gun. Can you maintain that vigilance 100% of the time?

If you see someone openly carrying a pistol they may be law abiding citizens exercising their rights…but for your own safety you need to regard them as a potential problem. You need to perceive them as (1) potential risk to your safety and the public, quickly followed by (2) a potential target for attack by others. You don't want to be standing next to some bullet magnet. Another issue that comes up, is one study has found people who open carry generally have never undergone any type of formal firearms training-not a good combination.

(COMPLETELY BIASED JUNK SCIENCE TACTICS TIP: IF YOU SEE A GUN IN A HOLSTER, THAT MAY BE A POSITIVE THING. CROOKS DON'T BOTHER TO BUY OR USE HOLSTERS!) Ask any policeman you know if they have ever taken a pistol off a criminal who had it in a holster.

DRAWING AGAINST THE DROP.

If you think you can fast draw into someone already pointing a gun at you-forget it. That is all the stuff of TV cowboy westerns. This is real life. The action vs reaction time just doesn't work in your favor. "But I have a really fast draw!" Better to angle away rapidly, drop or talk than try to "draw against the drop."

Something that needs to be pointed out here that may also rub your fur the wrong way…Pistols are not great weapons for having to shoot human beings to the point of submission. Clint Smith, famous firearm instructor and gun writer who said "You use a pistol to fight your way to a rifle or shotgun." People don't necessarily fall over dead just because they are shot, especially by a pistol.

They may also not stop being an aggressive, drunk or narcotics infected jerk just because they are shot. It may depend on the hydraulic pumping of unconfined blood, head trauma, skeletal breakdown, massive organ shock or extended amounts of time for the body to catch up with being shot by a pistol bullet.

Something on the order of 90% of human beings survive pistol wounds. Gun fight marksmanship is difficult at best.

So if you are realistically pinning all your hopes on a pistol for self-defense in an open carry holster gun without using some survival tactics and cover you are at a serious tactical and mental default.

WATCH THEIR HANDS. WATCH THEIR HANDS. WATCH THEIR HANDS. THEY ARE NOT GOING TO SHOOT YOU WITH THEIR EYES IF YOU ARE WATCHING FOR THOSE "CRAZY EYES."

AVOID THE ALTERCATION.

Much better to avoid the conflict in the first place, than to survive it via deadly force, and then be subjected to the American system of justice and the media. Here in 2017, even the police are being routinely grilled over media inflamed shootings and "outrages." Mega stress, mega expensive and you may lose your liberty.

You will also invariably see or hear this phrase again "EVERY BULLET HAS A LAWYER ATTACHED TO IT." People reviewing a gun involved incident will have months to gnaw on it, to listen to the media, to the outraged families on the nightly news saying what a good person the dead criminal was, and look for every angle to find blame and liability against you. You on the other hand will have short seconds to make those decisions.

Retreat or running away are both viable gun handling tactics. Your daily goal to return home at the end of the day alive makes you a gun fighter. Use all available strategic and tactical concepts to protect yourself and others. Rapid movement and running to cover or out of the target area are certainly viable survival tactics.

Are you willing to protect strangers? Are you going to protect them or rescue them? You don't know them, and you probably don't know what has led to the event that put them in danger. You may be at a severe tactical disadvantage not knowing who else is in the area that may initiate another attack upon you if you become involved. These are tough, multi-faceted problems for you to make with very little time or information to base your decisions upon. Better to avoid the problem if possible.

Many firearms trainers are teaching students to seek cover and defend themselves, call 911 and be a good witness versus interceding in deadly force situations they know little about.

It may be contrary to how you initially thought you would behave when you got a concealed carry permit, but carrying a gun is first and foremost designed to allow self-defense. It is OK to keep you as the number one priority and strangers come in further down the list.

CHAPTER EIGHT
WORKING WITHIN TIME.

Time is burning like a fuse. Don't wait until the explosion occurs before you start to react.

Real gunfights are not TV westerns with big hats and belt buckles (OK maybe where you live). For most of us, if you are thrust into a self-defense situation you need to incorporate the previously mentioned idea MOVE. If you are not actively shooting, you should be employing rapid movement and seeking some cover or concealment in conjunction with drawing and engaging with your gun. If you are still alive at that point, you can consider shooting or moving some more with a bit more ease...if you have time.

Time is an absolute reality-it is going to pass whether you are ready or not. If you have some pre-conceived ideas about what to do while that time is passing, and how to act in an emergency you can speed up your response as well as increase your survivability. Have some Action Plans already rehearsed and in your head..

On the cowboy shows, the good guy lets the bad guy go for his gun first and then because he is true of heart he is able to out draw and hit the bad guy with unerring accuracy.

You need to smash those ideas over the head with very real concepts of "Time". With gun incidents, time is rarely on your side, or in your favor, and if the bad guy is doing all the moving your chances of catching up are nil.

How fast can you draw your gun and hit a human sized target at a close to medium range with 100% accuracy? Two seconds? Three seconds? If you don't know, you should figure it out. Get someone to time you with a stopwatch or get a timer app on your smart phone to do it.

If things go bad, you have to think about it as you observe it, and then make decisions about what to do. It may take you four to ten seconds to realize something is wrong, then make decisions to do "something" and then start a draw sequence.

The actual drawing and shooting of a pistol is at the far back end of that time sequence. You might be standing, sitting or seat belted. You might be wearing clothing that prevents easy access to your gun. You may have other people around you. You may not have been paying attention and have shock or confusion built into the observation and reaction sequence. Many complicating factors are present when events are unravelling in short seconds.

In the event of a life threatening emergency, most of our high speed processing and decision making abilities can come to a near halt. Gross motor skills like draw and fire, flinch or jerk away from threat, still survive. Fine motor skills, like fumbling at buttons or zippers to get at your gun do not survive. Forget that one second draw and fire sequence from under your jacket or shirt...and heaven forbid you have an ankle holster on. You can time that draw and fire with a sun dial or a calendar.

In a high drama event, you may fall back on your training- if you have any prior training to fall back on. You must practice moving and drawing from your holster, aligning the sights and pressing the trigger. If you don't have access to a range, or lots of ammunition, dry fire techniques are just fine to build up some of that muscle memory.

If you hit the mental "Go" button for "Draw", you are catching some shortcuts in the burning time fuse problem. There are fewer decisions to be made if you have practiced drawing and moving.

WORKING INSIDE OF TIME-TICK TOCK, TICK TOCK.

The data you need to make decisions about going to guns or going to flight, arrives primarily through the eyes and some from your ears. It lands in the brain. Logic or cognitive powers in your brain try to make sense of what is being seen/heard.

You are "thinking and moving inside of time" and generally way behind in the Action vs Reaction curve. If they bad guy is already moving (Action) you need to get moving too (Reaction) but they have a jump on the passing seconds.

You and your favorite brain may be long seconds behind the action curve. How much bad stuff can go on in six seconds, ten seconds, twenty seconds?

KNIFE!

The best Action/Reaction training example involve facing a bad person with a knife. You should know the "21 FOOT

RULE" for knives. Here is the rule: <u>if a bad guy has a</u> <u>knife, you need at least 21 feet of distance and a barrier,</u> <u>between you and them to be able to minimally respond to a</u> <u>rushing attack.</u>

A committed attacker can cover up to 21 feet in about a second and a half. If there is no barrier between you and him, he can begin stabbing, slicing and dicing in even less than one and a half seconds and he does not have to reload.

This does not need to be a martial arts trained knife master. Pretty much any old human being can do it while your brain is still be stuck in the "Oh Shit" sequence. Even with a blazingly quick draw, you probably still have to think about making the draw after the person starts moving and you are at a definite time disadvantage. If you are six seconds away from drawing your gun you are gonna bleed...a lot. You need space and some barrier between you and a knife wielder.

You can look this entire knife attack sequence up on the internet and watch videos of trained policemen getting stabbed by attacking knife wielders in the street and in training, even when they probably know the attack is coming. They can rarely defend themselves in time.

21 feet seems like a long way away. Try it for yourself. Have someone come at you suddenly from that distance. Your hardwired first response to a rushing attack is generally to move backwards from the direction of attack. Bad guys know and profit from that response. They will mow you down as you retreat. On the street your second

response would usually involve starting to bleed and yelling alot.

When your mental gears mesh and recognize a rushing attack you must MOVE. Stepping laterally is contrary to where the bad guy thinks you will go, and it is hard for him to correct/redirect his rush to catch you.

In a You Tube video pasted below, Danny Inosanto, a legend in the martial arts community, and former student of Bruce Lee should should make a believer out of you about the danger of a knife attack.

https://www.youtube.com/watch?v=J_KJ1R2PCMM

https://www.youtube.com/watch?v=lk59imFr6yI

If you think you are going to use your Cobra-like reflexes in a rushing attack, then use your reflexes to jerk your body away or move out of target range. Get off the target X.

FLINCH!
Tony Blauer, a combatives trainer, came up with some very interesting hand to hand combat studies and found the unconscious and surprise "Flinch" response is the quickest human self-defense movement.

We all flinch if surprised by something suddenly coming at us like a door or a thrown object. Tony teaches a technique to use that flinch speed as part of self-defense. If you are taken by surprise, the flinch motion can be part of your movement out of the target area or throwing up your hands in defense. Hopefully it is an unexpected movement and not in a manner the bad guy would expect like merely backing up. Try plan to move at angles to a gun so that even if it goes off, you and many of your favorite organs won't be there.

If you can't do anything else at extreme close range you can flinch twist your torso to take your heart/lungs 45 degrees offline and knock at the gun with your hand or knife. The twist part is more important than hitting the gun. Even if it goes off you aren't standing square in front of it.

You would have to be in desperate straits to make that move. Generally your best moves would be to talk and/or move abruptly towards cover. One good thing in your favor in a gun fight situation is the fact bad guys are generally not very good marksmen. Couple that with your moving and running, and your odds just got much better than just standing still. It would literally be life or death decisions in that time bubble, but better to move, than let the bad guy decide what he is going to do to you in those critical seconds with you assuming the role as a static crash test dummy.

MOVE. MOVE. MOVE.

The time is going to pass-may as well fill it with movement and action. Even a small tactical move may pay dividends. Moving targets are infinitely harder to hit. Moving in time is even better-move and draw simultaneously, your brain already knows how to do it, like a flinch.

Real life fights involve twisting, turning, yelling, running and often involuntary movements to avoid getting shot, punched or stabbed. We don't get to practice moving and drawing at public shooting ranges, but you can practice to your heart's content at home.

Feel free to teach yourself this "Advanced Technique" and practice at home with an unloaded finger, empty and safe gun, a soft air gun or a BB gun, whatever you have. Step left while drawing and fire. Step right while drawing and fire. Try it forwards and backwards. It is less stable than getting braced like you are at a range, but works just fine at close to mid-range distances and you have the value added of moving in time. That time was going to pass anyway, tick-tock.

GUNSHOT SURVIVABILITY

Bad guys are notoriously poor shots. In 2016, in the most violent city in America, criminals shot 4378 human beings in Chicago. More than were shot in Afghanistan combat. Chicago had more people killed than in Los Angeles and New York City combined.

Only 762 of those shot in Chicago died of their gunshot wounds. These homicide numbers are horrific and are nearly double the 2015 totals, but everyone else survived. Poor marksmanship and the availability of rapid emergency medical assistance helped 3616 people survive.

People just don't keel over because they are shot. If you take on a sense of purpose you can continue to fight and even provide your own first-aid and not just lie down and die. Be a survivor. Expect to hurt but expect to fight and win.

The odds of surviving gunshot wounds in America are sky high especially when medical assistance is readily available.

Build into your head- "I am going to survive. If I am shot or shot at, I am going to get angry, and I am going to win against someone who dares attack me. I refuse to quit, and I am going home at the end of it all."

CREATIVE VISUALIZATION-REPEAT.

IF I AM SHOT I WILL NOT DIE. IF I AM SHOT I WILL NOT DIE.

I WILL CONTINUE TO FIGHT. I WILL CONTINUE TO FIGHT. I WILL CONTINUE TO FIGHT.

REPEAT THIS THREE TIMES. EMBED IT IN YOUR HEAD. BELIEVE IT. LIVE IT.

CHAPTER NINE
ACTIVE SHOOTER.

Unfortunately, here in 2017, we as law abiding citizens are quite worried about active shooters. We have seen tragedy after tragedy inflicted by bad guys upon helpless victims in America. The list goes on and on.

Most of us believe deep in our hearts, the only way to stop a bad guy with a gun is a good guy with a gun. We all believe we don't want to be in the position of having to live or die by the whim of a mentally deranged or religious belief or anger motivated active shooter or by the amount of ammunition they carry.

This chapter will provide facts and figures about active shooter events and methods as well as listing action plans.

This information may provide options when making traditional "Run-Hide-Fight" decisions which are being taught during active shooter training.

First and foremost, understand the average active shooter event lasts about 7-8 minutes. Some go longer, some shorter, but that is the current average. It does brace the old adage "When seconds count, the police are only minutes away."

In those 7-8 minutes you may be the only good guy with a gun on scene prior to law enforcement arrival. You will generally be facing multiple guns and lots of ammo brought by the bad guy and perhaps pipe bombs too. In a much smaller amount of events, there may even be two attackers. In a terrorism event there could be several bad guys.

You would only have your everyday carry gun and a reload if you brought one. You won't have any backup help, body armor and limited communications. You will also have a definite chance the responding police will target you if they arrive on scene before the bad guy is down. That is an awful tough scenario for anyone to willingly insert into even with a brave heart and good intentions.

Gun violence and gun deaths, are at their lowest rates in decades despite media portrayals, but active shooter events are on the rise.

The odds of being struck by lightning are much higher for you than being exposed to an active shooter or a spree shooter. Yet, it is one of the crimes that we as a society just cannot abide and gun owners guard against it despite the low odds of occurrence.

An "Active Shooter" is defined as one or more subjects actively engaged in causing death and/or great bodily harm. They may appear random or systematic, but it is generally marked by a spree characterized by their intent to continuously cause harm to innocent victims until stopped by police intervention or suicide.

Note: the large percentages of Spree Shooters kill themselves when confronted by armed police or citizens.

Be aware, if you confront them it may be enough for them to stop themselves permanently. A smaller number surrender when confronted and the smallest number are killed by police.

The spree shooter's overriding spree motivation is rage. It is about their internal rage and they see this shooting act as some sort of positive outlet. Their objective is to commit mass murder to bring them notoriety since the world has failed to see or celebrate how wonderful they are. They also likely suffer mental illness. These are not traditional criminal actors.

None of the liberal "common sense gun control plans" would have prevented or affected any of the most recent spree shootings and terror attacks, and in fact they actively look for "Gun Free Zones" to carry out their attacks.

When we see it on the news such an attack is beyond comprehension. The shock value and media hype adds to this feeling of wildness and adds to the fear that these shootings (truck driving/bombing/knifing/clubbing) are completely random and "It could happen anywhere."

However these acts are not random. They are carefully planned. Each and every time.

Every spree scene is extensively planned and designed to be chock full of potential victims to insure a huge body count. The locations, conditions, police presence and amount of public likely to be present as targets, are carefully screened to get maximum carnage and maximum publicity.

The shooters see themselves as going out in a blaze of glory like a comet burning out. They don't want any interference with their plans, and choose Gun Free Zones and helpless victims. They don't attack armed citizens or police stations. The Sandy Hook shooter chose kindergarten aged children as his targets-what could be even less able to defend themselves, fluffy puppies and kittens?

Harboring grudges, Spree Shooters have elaborate preparation, pre-attack surveillance, and gathering of guns, ammo and gear. Even worse, in every single case, studies after the fact have found the shooters leak their plans to people around them. Every single time. Columbine. Sandy Hook. Washington Navy Yard, Colorado Theater. Carolina Church Shooting. Wisconsin Sikh Temple. Chattanooga. San Bernardino. Orlando, Dallas.

Every event had people around the bad guy(s) who knew or suspected they were going to embark on a murder spree. People around them knew they were "not right."

Often times the shooters even post their actual plans and intentions in social media. In another disturbing trend this year they have been broadcasting live during the event with Facebook posts, Tweets and live video.

They boast of violent thoughts or fantasies to friends and family while overtly collecting weapons and making plans for the attack. The people around them don't want to believe it, and do nothing about it. "Oh it's just Kim Jong-Un, he's just kind of crazy and cranky. His daddy was cranky too. He doesn't really mean it. He'll be alright."

Other times, people see the bad guy getting worse and headed towards violence, but just don't know what to do about it. They don't want to call the police when no crime has occurred, and or don't want to get involved, or heaven forbid they do something to offend someone in this day and age.

No psychological profile fits every shooter, but they are all dealing with mental health issues, have a history of rage/depression or other issues, and probably have been treated with prescription drugs by medical professionals.

In many cases, they have made reoccurring suicide threats or suicidal behaviors that went unaddressed. They indulge in alcohol, illegal drugs and frequently have stopped taking therapeutic drugs. "I don't need them. I feel fine."

They are also all deteriorating in the days and weeks before they go berserk. Mentally they are slipping, and have extreme tunnel vision. They can only see their goal of reaching that blaze of glory and ending their pain and perceived insignificance. They don't take meds towards end, they don't sleep, and they don't eat or bathe or shave. Is it such a shock to learn three quarters of them have already unsuccessfully attempted suicide?

Planning and executing such vicious attacks which may include their own suicide at the end just does not make rational sense to rational beings.

Do understand when these deviants get locked into these self-absorbed delusions, it does not allow much self-editing or rational thought. Everything directed towards their big splash goal makes sense to them, and they are not asking anyone else "Hey does this sound crazy to you?" By the time they strike, they have isolated themselves and only have circular conversations in their own heads. They have pretty often written off the entire human race as having nothing in common with them.

Additional terror/shooter characteristics which are different than criminals characteristics, is negotiation is unlikely, and victims get no sympathy and little interaction. They don't want to rob them, beat them or have sex with them-they don't want anything from victims except for them to die in furtherance of their fantasy of the glory they will garner.

Active shooters seek media attention while criminals don't. Criminal gunmen would prefer remote locations and no witnesses to carry out their crimes. Spree Shooters want public statements of their unhappy lives to as large an audience as possible.

US Secret Service Threat Assessment Center published some recent data on studies and not surprisingly found active shooter incidents are rarely impulsive. They are well thought out plans of attack and 75% planned the attack ahead of time and gathered gear ahead of time. 50% had revenge as a motive. 66% of the weapons used came from their home or that of a relative. In 75% of the incidents an adult had already expressed concerns about the attacker before the attack. 75% had either attempted or threatened to commit suicide

In a published FBI study in 2014, they stated Active Shooter incidents have doubled in the last seven years. It seems like so much more than that, with all of the media attention which includes real time exposure to international events and audiences.

In 2000-2013, the FBI studied 160 active shooter incidents. 1043 casualties. 486 died/558 wounded. In the last seven years preceding 2014 they saw on average 16.4 incidents per year. Of those, 154 of 160 incidents were male shooters (only two involved more than one shooter).

In more than half of the incidents, (90 shootings) ended on the shooter's initiative (i.e., suicide, fleeing), while 21 incidents ended after unarmed citizens successfully restrained the shooter. That is a pretty big number for unarmed citizens to have intervened in light of the savage firepower the bad guys are bringing to the scene. Law enforcement engaged 45 shooters. In 21 incidents, nine officers were killed and 28 were wounded.

In rough terms officers were killed in one out of five such incidents and an officer was wounded in more than half of those incidents.

For concealed carriers, you need to realize if you choose to engage there is a very real chance of being injured. Is that 50/50 chance worth noting? Yes it is. We don't ordinarily think about ourselves getting hurt in our "I'll stop that guy" dream. We don't ordinarily include self-applied first aid in our concealed carry plans.

The FBI study saw event locations to include Commercial Buildings 45.6 percent (73 incidents), Educational Buildings 24.3 percent, (39 incidents). The remaining incidents occurred at other location types specified in the study—open spaces, military and other government properties, residential properties, houses of worship, and health care facilities.

ACTION PLAN-RESPONSE TO ACTIVE SHOOTER

RUN-HIDE-FIGHT

In the event of spree shooting best practice is to run away (escape), if you are not able to flee then hide, and finally if no other option exists prepare to fight for your life and/or the lives of other human beings.

It is not recommended by law enforcement in general that you run towards the sounds of consistent firing in an attempt to stop it, even though you have a gun. Protect yourself and others, and leave the scene.

If you choose to engage use cover/concealment, and good tactics. Cheat if you can! As a single gun carrier with no immediate backup you are in a 7 to 8 minute event without backup. As stated above, the bad guy(s) will generally have several guns- to include rifles and shotguns, lots of ammunition, and may have homemade bombs.

 Any bad guy(s) you choose to confront will be only after they have made elaborate plans and you will have only your gun and any extra bullets on your person until police help arrives. You won't have any bullet resistant clothing, extra ammo, handcuffs or first aid supplies in that time frame or medical help until things calm down with reinforcements arriving.

ACTIVE SHOOTER ACTION PLAN #1
EVACUATE/RUN

If there is an accessible escape path, attempt to evacuate the premises (windows, doors).

Stay low and quiet.

Move fast-moving targets are difficult to shoot.

Be sure to have an escape route and plan in mind.

Look for lighted EXIT signs if you do not know the building layout.

Evacuate regardless of whether others agree to follow.

Just like a grade school fire drill, leave your belongings behind.

Help others escape, if possible.

It is very difficult to move wounded people. Dead weight is dead weight. You may have to escape to save yourself.

Prevent individuals from entering an area where the active shooter may be

Call 911 when you are safe

Understand if you are running with your gun displayed, you may become a police target

ACTION PLAN #2 HIDE

If evacuation is not possible, find a place to hide where the active shooter is less likely to find you.

Assume barricade position with your firearm out. Be out of the active shooter's view, cover inset door windows.

Do not expose any more of your body than absolutely necessary in a firing position.

Seek Cover and Concealment in case shots are fired in your direction (i.e., a closed and locked door). Bricks better than wood. Wood/metal better than drywall.

Avoid trapping yourself if possible-is there a window which can be used for a non-traditional exit?

Lock the door; tie the door down with belts, electrical cords or curtain cords. If it opens inward, shim or wedge material at the bottom in an improvised door stop.

Blockade the door with heavy furniture.

Help the injured.

Remain quiet and hidden until police arrive and call out looking for survivors

SURVIVING RICOCHETS

Bullets striking the floor or walls at flat angles tend to continue to fly parallel with the flat surface (about 6 inches away). Hugging the wall or flat on floor is not recommended. Crouch, don't press up against the wall or lie flat on floor if you are out in the open.

SURVIVING EXPLOSIVES

Shrapnel from grenades, propane bombs or pipe bombs tend to go up and out.

In bomb attacks, dive away face down with feet towards the explosive, elbows by ribs, cover ears, close eyes, open mouth. Do not look immediately towards explosions near buildings--flying glass can wound/blind. It is a human response to look towards an explosion. Teach yourself to equate explosion with flinch response lowering your head for several seconds instead of immediately looking towards the source of the explosion.

ACTION PLAN #3 FIGHT TO SAVE YOUR LIFE

No ability to escape or hide. Fight as your last resort.
Believe-YOU MUST WIN. It may be a fight for your very life.

"If I am shot I will not die. If I am shot I will not die. If I am shot I will not die. I will fight. I will fight. I will fight. I am going home to my family."

Deliberate aimed shots can win the day. Don't spray and pray.

Bad guys frequently kill themselves when confronted by guns or police.

Attempt to disrupt/distract, blind or incapacitate the active shooter. Throw, kick, stab, punch.

Plan your attack with overwhelming force until you win. Acting as aggressively as possible. Suspect may retreat even if armed.

Throw items. Club, flail, whip, stab. Use improvised weapons like furniture, water bottles, books, scissors, staplers, pens, computers, screwdriver, discharge fire extinguisher etc.

Fight dirty, attack as a group.

LAW ENFORCEMENT ARRIVES

Insure you don't have your gun in your hand when police arrive or confront you. If you are holding and pointing a gun towards police or anyone else during an active shooter situation, the police will shoot you. It would be nice if there was time to call out "Put the gun down" but it may not happen as they are trained to stop shooters as soon as possible to save lives.

Officers will proceed directly to the area in which the last shots were heard. They will have to ignore wounded people during initial entry. Area control and shooter control is first priority to save lives. This looks and seems callous, but active shooter protocols have evolved from the Columbine days where they surrounded the school and waited for back-up officers to arrive. In the meantime kids were dying inside that school. Now, when officers arrive at shots fired calls, they go immediately towards the shooter to stop further loss of life. They know they are working with the same seven or eight minute window you are. In the big city you can get a lot of officers on scene quickly. In more suburb or rural areas everyone will come for miles around, but it will take more time. If your small or medium town only has 4 officers on per shift or you are in an unincorporated area covered by the Sheriff's Office, it is just going to take more time to get forces there.

Officers may wear regular patrol uniforms or external bulletproof vests, Kevlar helmets, and other tactical equipment. Officers may not be in uniform. Police broadcast of public shootings will bring in every law officer for miles, some will come from home. Bad guys have worn real body armor and other times have worn assault vests with lots of pockets full of magazines that look like body armor-they may look like off duty cops or plain clothes cops who threw on a vest from the trunk of their car to respond.

Officers may be armed with rifles, shotguns, handguns. They may use pepper spray or tear gas to control the situation. Officers will shout commands, and push individuals to the ground roughly- it is for both parties safety. You may be handcuffed. Don't fight or struggle against it. That may be a good time to announce "I have a concealed carry permit and my firearm is on my hip."

Remain calm, and obey officers. Put down any items in your hands (i.e., bags, jackets). Immediately raise hands and spread fingers. Keep hands visible at all times. They do not know who is a suspect and who is not a suspect. Avoid making quick movements toward officers such as rushing, grabbing or holding on to them. Avoid pointing, screaming and/or yelling-they are already keyed up enough. You don't want to push them in to panic mode.

People will be evacuated out of the building/area to a safe location. They will be sorted out there prior to release. It takes time to go through that portion because there are so many moving parts and responding officers to an event like this. People will have to be interviewed and screened to gather information on what they saw in the scene. That part can take a lot of time, but you aren't being shot at anymore so just go with it ok?

CHAPTER TEN
FIREARM SAFETY-PERSONAL CARRY, HOME, VEHICLE AND IN PUBLIC.

Reading all of the state statues associated with Illinois concealed carry, it is quite evident the legislators pushed through laws which are very stringent about protecting the public at all times from wanton acts of firearms violence or accident.

Every state that ever considered and passed a concealed carry law went through the same concerns. There have always been critics who decried there would be blood running in the streets if more people were carrying guns- and yet it has never happened.

They don't address the fact the applicants are law abiding citizens willing to undergo training and education and heavy fees to be able to exercise their rights in a lawful manner- it is criminals who don't follow the laws.

The legislatures also don't address the fact it is already a crime in every state to misuse a firearm or use one to further any other crime. It may even be a federal offense to abuse firearms in this manner. Instead, the legislators especially those representing large cities, feared break outs of "old west" shootings in the street or vigilante justice. But it has never happened.

John Lott, a college professor and researcher, conducted an academic study to see what could be statistically proven where more legal guns are present (like through issuance of concealed weapons licenses) and any effect on crime rates.

Professor Lott's excellent book "More Guns Less Crime" published his results, and he found crime rates receded in every state where data was available. Law abiding gun owners and concealed carry license holders were exactly that-law abiding citizens. The flood of old west shootings in the street has never materialized-in any state in the nation and crime rates went down in every location where concealed carry permits were added to state laws.

The Lott books have been wildly criticized by every corner of the liberal media, "researchers" and "academics" who are supposed peers of Lott. Yet his studies have not been broken, and many of the critics who went public with their assertions have been documented to have never even read the book.

The Lott books are highly recommended reading to help develop an understanding on concealed carry laws and studies, but also to see the lengths anti-gun critics will go to try and bury gun laws and gun owners. Every gun owner and Concealed Carry License holder should be well versed in the real facts associated with the Second Amendment and gun rights.

FIREARM SAFETY

This broad topic includes the safe handling of guns at home and afield, but also includes the safety of each gun handler, people near them or people they may come in contact with when they are exercising their rights to concealed carry.

Two types of hand held firearms will be addressed in the teaching portions of this book, pistols and revolvers.

Pistols are semi-automatic handguns which have a magazine of ammunition inserted into the magazine well. The cycle of operation involves retracting the slide which cocks the hammer or striker and allowing a loaded cartridge to push up in the magazine. Releasing the slide allows the breach to push the top round off of the magazine forward into the chamber and the slide locks into battery. When the gun is fired the slide retracts sharply, extracts the now empty shell casing from the chamber of the barrel and pulls it rearward until it strikes the ejector which causes the empty brass to fly out of the breech. The slide pushes back forward and picks up the next loaded cartridge from the top of the magazine and pushes it into the chamber. This completes the cycle of operations for a semi-automatic pistol.

A revolver has the dominant revolving cylinder in the middle of the gun which may hold five, six, eight or even ten cartridges depending upon model and caliber. A latch on the exterior of the gun is pressed and the cylinder is pushed towards the left side of the gun and it swings open to expose the entire cylinder. Ammunition is loaded and unloaded from the exposed cylinder. Closing the cylinder into the frame of the gun and rotating it slightly until it clicks or stops movement places the gun into battery. If the trigger is then pulled the cylinder will rotate one position to the left or right (depending on make and model) aligning a cartridge with the barrel. Continued pull on the trigger raises the hammer off of the rear of the frame, moves it rearward and then it falls forward to strike or cause an intervening piece of the gun to strike the primer of the cartridge in line with the barrel causing a detonation. There is no other movement in the cycle of action for a revolver.

All four of the universal gun safety topics cited at the beginning of this book must be incorporated with all gun handling, storage and use no matter if it is a pistol or revolver. At law, a strict liability tort is the kind of action which is so inherently dangerous it automatically must hold the actor accountable for any bad conduct or damage which results. The media and many lawsuits try to hold gun owners and even gun manufacturers liable for all bad acts committed with a firearm and claim guns are inherently dangerous.

No other items available for public consumption are treated so harshly in our society. Doctors, automobiles and drunk drivers kill more people than any other causes in the U.S. Even bathtub drowning far outnumber firearms deaths, but there are no public crusades or big city mayors shouting for doctor registration, vehicle control, liquor controls or demands for bath tub registration.

These nearly fanatical accusations are leveled at guns and gun owners on a regular basis. Despite the fact gun crime and gun accidents are on a steadily receding decline for years now, with every shooting headline there are calls for stricter laws. Like Chicago…where they have the strictest gun laws and highest shooting and murder rate in the U.S. Turns out criminals don't follow the law.

Media sources and critics ignore the fact guns have always been a key ingredient to our continued free society and are used by private citizens up to one million times a year in self-defense where no one is killed.

Firearms were deemed important enough by the framers of the Constitution to be addressed in the second amendment to the first ten amendments to the Constitutional document –known to all as "The Bill of Rights". The only items of personal property mentioned in the Constitution are personal papers and effects. Guns were deliberately listed by the framers.

Recent court cases including U.S. Supreme Court cases have found the right to keep and bear arms applies to the individual citizens not just to militias. The right may be regulated and taxed, or have public safety requirements attached to it-but the right to keep and bear arms cannot be completely withheld from the general public by state or local legislative bodies.

The City of New York, District of Columbia and City of Chicago all had absolute bans on firearms possession for many years-yet they all had terrible and internationally known murder rates year after year. The criminals did not obey the laws-only the good citizens obeyed the law and were then kept unarmed by the good intentions of their legislators who erroneously believed all guns are bad and more guns equate with more crime.

With all of this in mind, the person who seeks out and obtains a concealed carry license needs to know their possession and use of a firearm incur obligations to absolutely conduct themselves in the safest possible manner for their own safety, their family's safety and the public safety. Any hint of abuse will be touted in the media, reviewed for prosecution and open the gun handler to civil law suits as well.

SHOOTING PRACTICE AND RANGE SAFETY

There are phrases throughout the law enforcement and military that "you fight like you train". Out of this concept, gun carriers should view practicing with their firearm in a serious training mindset. Focused practice benefits the shooter much more than simple "plinking". Practice skills, movements and reloads in a manner you may one day be called upon to utilize in an emergency.

All firearm practice should include the four safety rules and using the holster and ammunition carriers and even clothing they will use or carry in the street.

Recall once again the four safety rules: #1 treat the gun as if it is always loaded, #2 keep finger off the trigger until ready to shoot, #3 never pointing the firearm at something you are not willing to shoot or destroy (muzzle awareness) and #4 be aware of backstops and beyond. These rules are just as valid at home, in a vehicle, in public or on a shooting range.

In addition to the four safety rules above, eye and hearing conservation cannot be overstated in conjunction with firearm practice. Many old and now deaf shooters started shooting when hearing conservation was never considered. Some of the early attempts to deal with noise were shooters putting cigarette filters or empty brass casings in their ear canals....ridiculous but true stories that did not work! The damaged ear canal nerve endings never regenerate.

Today all firearms instructors insist on some type of modern hearing protection, and most (especially indoors range and rifle shooting) insist on double hearing protection using soft roll up puffs which expand inside the ear canal-covered by hard shell hearing protectors.

NEVER SHOOT FIREARMS IN A PRACTICE SESSION WITHOUT HEARING PROTECTION IN PLACE.

Soft roll up type protection cost only pennies and should be thrown away after a single use. They have Noise Rate Reduction (NRR) levels around 19-22 Decibels (dB). Hard shell muffs are reusable and have NRR ratings from 19-29 db. Combining the soft and hard protectors does not automatically double the NRR, but provides considerable extra protection, especially when the hard shell muffs are old or do not fit well.

Some shooters prefer hard shell muffs that have connecting straps that can slip over the top of the head or behind the neck. The behind the neck application is comfortable, but shooters should be aware this placement may drop the effective NRR by 10 dB. Having soft roll up type plugs combined with the neck strap position will help offset some of that loss.

There are many different types of hearing protections on the market and when asked which is best, an audiologist once stated "The one that is in your ears at the time you need it".

The NRR ratings are apparently somewhat open to interpretation, so get the best protection you can and using it in high noise areas will be your best chance to avoid high range hearing loss and permanent damage-and certainly any protection is better than no protection.

Cheap rubber flanged plugs are comfortable and issued by the military in conjunction with hard shell earmuffs. There are similar in-ear plugs with baffles which claim to allow normal conversation but seal up with loud noise blasts. Consumers should double check these types of plugs as their NRR may only be 9-12 Db.

Electronic hearing protection has developed over the last twenty years or so to provide very effective and inexpensive protection. The electronic muffs are battery operated hard shell muffs which have microphone(s) which do broadcast normal conversations to the wearer's ears. When loud noise is detected over 100db (in the pain producing range) the muffs have an electronic circuit click off the microphones in a micro-second to protect the wearer. When the blast subsides, the microphones turn back on and normal conversation can be heard again.

These muffs can run from $20-$200 depending on manufacturer and features. Mid-range muffs like Peltor brand may run from $50-$75 and are very popular with competition shooters for their stereo microphones, quality sound and slim profile design which works well with shooting rifles and shotguns (older styled rounded hard muffs may not fit well up against butt stocks.) Electronic muffs are especially helpful for gun students and instructors being able to communicate on noisy ranges in between loud noises.

Tactically, the use of electronic muffs has even been advocated by gun magazine writers who have hearing loss (as is very common with older shooters who did not grow up in a generation that demanded hearing protection). The gun writers have spoken of putting on electronic muffs at home with the listening volume on high while checking out

91

possible intruders in the home since they can hear more noise with the muffs on and active than they can with their firearm deafened ears can unaided.

EYE PROTECTION-ALWAYS WEAR EYE PROTECTION WHEN PRACTICING WITH FIREARMS

This is even more important than hearing protection-you only have two eyes. If you go deaf you might get a hearing aid that can help you. If you go blind or lose one eye that will be a loss which lasts forever.

Consider eye and hearing protection to go hand in hand with firearms practice. You must wear quality eye protection to prevent ammunition explosions, or ricochets from impacting your eyes. If you shoot enough guns, enough times in enough situations, you will most likely eventually receive some sort of unintentional blow back, debris or impact in the face. Having quality eye protection which covers the eye socket, will greatly decrease the chance of serious damage.

Obtain and use high impact lens shooting or safety glasses-ordinary sunglasses may not provide impact protection or cover the eye orbits sufficiently. Sporting goods stores sell many brands of shooting protection glasses and hardware/home improvement stores also carry impact rated safety glasses in clear, yellow or sunshade lenses at very reasonable prices.

For those shooters who wear eye glasses, they probably have drop resistant/impact resistant lenses, but they do not wrap around the brow/temple like safety glasses do. Plastic side shields may be obtained that slip on the glasses bow to provide side coverage in addition to the front coverage. Another choice is to put safety glasses over smaller normal glasses to provide the additional coverage.

ADDITIONAL RANGE AND PERSONAL SAFETY RULES.

Keep a weapon pointed in a safe direction at all times-be muzzle conscious at all times even if the gun is thought to be unloaded and set on a bench.

Do not handle any weapons while anyone is downrange or in front of you.

Never draw the weapon with your finger on the trigger. Holsters should have covered trigger guards. Always inspect any potential holster for this feature to prevent a trigger finger being inserted during the draw or the trigger getting moved by something intruding into the trigger area like brush or zippers or drawstrings which may push or pull on the trigger. Only place your finger on the trigger if you are ready to shoot.

Do not turn around while you are on a range with a gun in your hand. If you need to move with the gun, holster it, unload it, bench it or point the muzzle at the ground.

Do not holster single action pistols (like cowboy style pistols) or pistols that do not have an external safety with the hammer pulled to the rear unless the safety is engaged (like 1911 style .45's and some Beretta and Ruger pistols.)

When shooting for practice, do not place ammunition in front of you or and not shoot over ammunition on a bench. Keep ammunition to the side or behind the weapon.

Learn to holster your weapon with one hand. Shooters often reach across with their free hand to assist holstering and unintentionally "laser" or point the muzzle at their free hand in doing so.

Concentrate on shooting when you are practicing, and do not eat or drink, listen to music or use cell phones on the range. All of these things detract from the shooters concentration and attention given to the proper use of firearms and safety rules.

When you leave a practice session insure any gun you are putting in a case is unloaded. Open the action and inspect the chamber visually and physically check with a finger to insure it is unloaded. Look away and do it again before putting a weapon away.

Weapon malfunctions occur from time to time and for a variety of reasons. The use of well-made modern firearms and ammunition will lessen the chances of malfunctions but cannot prevent every possibility. Another simple procedure to help prevent malfunctions is to have your weapon cleaned after each practice session and lubricated. This is especially important with semi-automatic pistols.

Some malfunctions can be caused by ordinary wear and tear-parts wear down and magazine feed lips get bent. Some problems may be attributed to faulty ammunition and some other problems can be attributed to the shooters themselves.

If you have a problem with your firearm or ammunition, clear the weapon so it is empty and safe and then look for gouges, cracks, missing or broken parts.

Most semi-automatic pistols are made to be handled with the maximum amount of spring tension and spring release, so when dropping or releasing the slide let it slam home-it will not detonate the loaded bullet and is designed to operate this way. Do not hold the back end of the slide with your off hand and slowly ride it forward-this is a high probability way to institute a jam or malfunction.

Immediate Action and Secondary Immediate Action Drills to clear malfunctions will be addressed elsewhere, but simply put; if a revolver does not fire pull the trigger again. The cylinder should revolve, the hammer cycle and detonate the next round.

If a semi-automatic pistol does not fire when expected the Immediate Action Drill is to TAP the base of the magazine to insure it is seated. RACK the slide to clear the chamber of any fouled round and insert a new round, and READY-reassess the shooting area to see if it still safe to shoot. This drill will clear most malfunctions and was formerly known as TAP/RACK/BANG. If the gun does not fire the second time, the secondary drill is to RIP the magazine out, WORK the action two or three times, insert a new magazine and TAP the base to insure it is seated, RACK the slide back and release it to slam home and READY-reassess the shooting area to see if it is still safe to shoot. This secondary immediate action drill was formerly known as RIP/WORK/TAP/RACK/BANG.

If you fire a round of ammunition and do not receive the expected amount of recoil or the sound is much smaller than anticipated (like a "pop" vs a "boom") stop firing immediately. You may have just experienced a "Squib" load-or a load that did not perform correctly, did not have the correct amount of powder or even be the wrong ammunition for the gun (a frequent example is shooting 9mm ammunition in a .40 pistol-the round may chamber and detonate but it sounds puny and has little felt recoil compared to the .40 round).

Squib rounds are usually underpowered, and may actually not be powerful enough to have the bullet leave the barrel. The lands and grooves inside a barrel actually are quite tight and the bullet could be lodged inside the barrel and if a second shot if fired the second bullet and gases will push up against the obstruction and create an overpressure inside the barrel that is quite dangerous and could rupture the barrel.

If a squib round is suspected, cease fire immediately. Remove all ammunition from the weapon and clear the chamber area. The barrel will have to be visually inspected or a cleaning rod inserted to insure there is no bullet lodged in the bore so it is imperative the gun be absolutely unloaded and made safe before inspecting the barrel. With semi-automatic guns it is a good idea to remove the slide and barrel from the frame and inspect the barrel when it is removed from the slide. With a revolver, open the cylinder up, clear any brass or loaded cartridges out of the cylinder and then inspect the barrel with the cylinder held open and out of the frame.

Reloaded ammunition is a frequent source of squib loads, but even brand name factory ammunition can produce rounds which do not fire correctly. Loads may even be found which do not have any powder in the casing. In those examples the primer has enough force to send the bullet into the barrel and frequently does not exit the barrel. Faulty primers may not have enough fire to ignite the powder, and very old powder or powder that has been exposed to penetrating moisture may not ignite and cause a squib malfunction as well.

IF YOU HAVE A ROUND FAIL TO FIRE-LEAVE THE GUN FACING DOWN RANGE FOR AT LEAST 30 SECONDS. AFTER CLEARING DO NOT PLACE THE ROUND IN YOUR POCKET-A REMOTE CHANCE REMAINS THE POWDER COULD STILL IGNITE. SET THE ROUND ASIDE AND DISPOSE OF IT AT THE END OF YOUR RANGE SESSION.

Another range safety issue likely to be encountered by every shooter eventually is a ricochet or pieces of fragmented bullets bouncing back from the target area, bullet trap or backstop. Shooting into outdoor backstops with large rocks or shooting target grade steel targets increase the chances of this type of impact. Shooters may have fragments or pieces of ricochets strike their face, hands or body-some may hurt or inflict bleeding injuries if sharp metal jackets cut the skin. These instances are fairly rare and usually minor contacts; however, once again, constant use of eye protection while shooting will prevent eye injury. If a ricochet or fragment cuts the skin, be sure to clean the area with soap and water to prevent infection.

Hot expended brass is another unpleasant but regular part of shooting, especially at indoor ranges where shooters are set up in parallel booths and ejected brass may fly over the partition and land on the neighboring shooter or go inside their clothing. This expended brass is very hot for several seconds and if it falls inside the collar of a shirt "the hot brass dance" may occur trying to get the burning item out of the shooter's shirt. It is critical to know the brass is hot and burns, but it will not kill you, and it is far less dangerous than dancing around waiving a loaded gun while trying to get the offending cartridge out.

If hot brass falls inside clothing, put your weapon down or holster it before using your weapon hand to try and remove the hot brass. Wrap around eye glasses help prevent hot brass from getting caught in the eye orbit as do ball caps with long brims. Some shooters wear collared shirts with the shirt buttoned all the way up or with the collar turned up to try and prevent brass from other shooters dropping in.

Being aware in advance of possible hot brass falling into your clothing won't make it burn any less, but hopefully you can program a response into your brain to deal with it safely and not cause further risk to yourself or others while trying to clear the brass from your clothing.

ON RANGE AND OFF RANGE WEAPON HANDLING

Remember always treat every weapon as if it is loaded. Any time you handle a weapon point it in the safest possible direction, open the action or cylinder and visually and physically inspect the firearm to make sure it is unloaded. Never rely upon "I always leave it unloaded" or your memory of the condition of the weapon you last handled it-treat it as if it is loaded any time you handle it until you have visually and physically inspected the weapon.

With these same tenets in mind, handing a weapon over to another person or having a weapon handed to you is a potentially dangerous act. Do not hand it over until you have inspected the weapon to insure it does not contain any ammunition. Lock the action open or open the cylinder before handing it over.

By the same measure, if you are handed a weapon and someone says "Don't worry, it is not loaded", do not assume it is empty or safe. **ASSUME EVERY WEAPON IS LOADED**. Point it in a safe direction and open the action to insure it is not in fact loaded. If it is a weapon you are not familiar with you can decline to receive it or ask the other person to open the chamber to show you how the weapon works so you may inspect the chamber yourself. People get shot accidentally by "Don't worry, it is not loaded" guns and they are all preventable accidents.

SAFE TRANSFERS OF WEAPONS FROM PERSON TO PERSON

On the range, shooters frequently share a weapon. If the weapon is still loaded, it is permissible to bench the weapon or even place it on the ground facing in the safest direction and moving away from it before the second shooter takes control. Verbally state "It is loaded" so there is no confusion about the condition of the weapon. Insure the barrel remains pointed down range. It is much safer to take a few seconds to unload the weapon before allowing another person to take control. Handing a weapon to another person should best be conducted with an unloaded and safe weapon.

Revolver – place the weapon in the non-shooting hand with fingers and thumb around the cylinder (not on the trigger), press on the cylinder with strong hand and push the cylinder out of the frame with fingers of the weak hand. Slide the weak hand fingers through the open frame and grasp the cylinder. Actual passing of the gun involves handing it grip first while keeping the cylinder out of the frame.

Semi-auto pistols are more complicated. First remove the source of ammunition while keeping the muzzle pointed in a safe direction. This insures any further manipulation of the action will not simply eject a live round from the chamber and insert another round from the magazine. With the magazine removed the maximum number of rounds inside the pistol should be one-the round in the chamber. Lock the slide to the rear-this should eject any round left inside the chamber/barrel. Visually and physically inspect the chamber/barrel area to insure no round is left in there. Also look down through the action towards the floor-the magazine area in the butt of the gun should be empty with no mag or stray bullet remaining in that area. Only then is it safe to transfer a semi-auto pistol to another person by holding it muzzle down and butt first to the person receiving it.

PISTOL SAFETIES

There are many different kinds of pistols and revolvers developed over the last couple of hundred years and many have unique actions involved with their firing sequence and have many different mechanical devices which may or may not be called "safeties".

The only real safety is between your ears. The gun handler is the ultimate safety. If they treat a weapon with respect and keep the big four safety rules in mind at all times they are "safe" no matter what mechanical safeties are installed on the device.

Old black powder guns required a loading process that included pouring powder down the bore, then stuffing a lead ball on top and either a pan of loose powder and a flint for ignition or a small copper cap that would fire when struck by the hammer. The several steps to make the gun ready were all pretty safe features.

Black powder revolvers evolved before the American civil war to contain six chambers but had to be loaded with powder and a ball or bullet and a percussion cap placed on the back end of the cylinder. Without percussion caps in place these guns would be pretty safe to handle and move around. But it is still a "loaded weapon."

Revolvers next evolved into single action cowboy style guns and double action revolvers with metallic cartridge shells that contain the powder and a primer embedded in the base takes the place of the old separate percussion cap. A bullet is seated in the casing and the round is self-contained, very stable and largely weather resistant.

The old Colt single action cowboy style gun was a very accurate, very dependable large caliber handgun, but there was no independent safety on the gun. With a loaded cylinder and the hammer down, an impact upon the hammer or even a fall could cause the hammer to create an impact that would cause a primer to detonate and fire the gun. In the old west, responsible gun handlers learned to only keep five rounds in the cylinder and the hammer centered over the empty chamber. This trait continued into this century and remains a good safety practice with this type of gun.

Some modern redesigns like the Ruger line have incorporated an interrupting drop safety that will prevent the hammer unintentionally impacting and detonating a round. It is important to know if your weapon has this feature installed. It is usually easily researched via the internet or with a call to the gun's manufacturer before you carry it.

The old cowboy style guns are known as "single action" guns as you have to thumb the hammer back before each shot. There is no mechanical device that will cock the hammer for you. If the hammer is down and you pull the trigger the hammer does not move.

Modern revolvers do not have external safeties. If you pull the trigger, the hammer will cock to the rear and then fall forward and detonate a cartridge-this is known as "double action". The safest part of the modern revolver is the long trigger pull known as double action. You can also thumb the hammer back on a revolver (making it a single action feature) and shoot it with a short trigger pull with much less effort. This is an inherently more dangerous condition for a revolver to be in. **Never carry or holster a revolver with the hammer cocked to the rear.**

Semi-automatic pistols or self-loading pistols did not originate with the John M. Browning designed 1911 .45ACP pistol, but it is the most famous and probably the most prolific pistol with an external safety built in.

There is a safety switch located on the left rear of the 1911 slide which is engaged with the thumb if you hold the gun in the right hand. The gun is safe to carry with the hammer down on a live chamber, but it cannot fire in that condition. There is no double action mechanism that will pull the hammer to the rear like a revolver.

To fire, a 1911 it must have the hammer retracted at some point, the slide safety in the off position and a separate safety toggle on the back of the pistol grip has to be depressed with the web of the hand all before the trigger can be pulled. The 1911 is a "single action" pistol in that the hammer has to be cocked in advance to fire it. Cycling of the firing sequence re-cocks the hammer each time and it does not have to be thumbed back each time.

The grip safety on the 1911 is fairly unique to that pistol. You must be holding it tightly in one hand against the web of the hand to disengage that safety. Pressing on the trigger without first depressing the grip safety will not let the hammer drop. John Browning did not include the grip safety in his next big innovation pistol the Browning Hi-Power 9mm, but it continues on all modern 1911's to this day built by Colt, Kimber, Springfield Armory and other well-known manufacturers.

The slide mounted safety is thumb manipulated up and down to lock the trigger and hammer. It is safe to carry a loaded 1911 .45 with the hammer back and slide mounted safety engaged. This is known as "Cocked and Locked".

To a non-gun savvy observer seeing a .45 with the hammer back in a holster it looks openly dangerous-but it is not. The gun was designed to be carried in this manner and has been carried this way since it was put into government inventory just before WWI.

The 1911 remains one of the best combat and self-defense handguns ever developed. It is still in vogue with high speed law enforcement units like LAPD SWAT and FBI HRT and with some elite military units. It was the American military pistol from WWI until replaced by the Beretta 9mm pistol in the 1990s. The current military Beretta model, the 92F or M9 also has a slide mounted thumb activated safety similar to the 1911. (Several other Beretta models have different safety systems, but the military model still has the slide mounted safety on it).

Double Action Only (DAO) semi-automatics have evolved away from the Double/Single action combination triggers found on semi-automatics like Sig's, Rugers, Berettas and they function just like a revolver trigger. The DAO hammer is at rest in the down position, and pulling the trigger raises and cocks the hammer and then releases it to fall forward and strike the firing pin. The gun cannot be hand cocked or have the hammer cocked back at any time.

The DAO trigger pull matches the revolver double action pull and is touted as being "safer" because it has a long and heavy pull to make the gun function. The trigger pull weight and feel is the same with every trigger pull. This is different than guns with both a double and single action which have a long double action pull for the first shot but much lighter trigger pull for each respective shot.

The makers of the Double Action Only (or DAO) guns claim they are also easier to train with since each trigger pull is the same as the last. Smith and Wesson, Ruger, Beretta and others build their stock guns with the option of having a DAO trigger. Sig Sauer has something very similar called a DAK trigger which operates like a DAO trigger. DAO guns do not have an external safety on the side.

Striker Fired pistols are something wholly different from the double/single actions or the DAOs. Glocks are the best known of this type of action. Springfield makes the XD and XDM in striker fired actions. Glock markets their trigger as "safe action" instead of single action or double action. The amount of pressure to activate the trigger remains the same from shot to shot like a DAO gun, however, the travel distance and amount of pressure is much less than a DAO.

A DAO gun may take 12 lbs of pressure to fire, whereas the Glock only takes 5lbs of pressure to fire. Once again, there are no external safeties on the Glock or the XD's and the function of the trigger and some internal safeties still make these very safe weapons.

On the outside the Glock has a "trigger safety" which is a small tongue that extends out of the front of the trigger. Pressing directly upon the trigger depresses the tongue and makes the weapon able to fire. Like the grip safety on 1911 guns, if there is no direct pressure on the trigger safety the gun will not fire and ostensibly dragging or side pressure on the rest of the trigger will not allow the trigger to depress. Glocks also have drop safeties internally which prevent the gun from firing if dropped from a height.

PERSONAL CARRY SAFETY

Get a holster. If you are going to carry a pistol on your person get a good quality holster to secure the weapon. A later chapter will discuss types of holsters and their advantages, but from a safety standpoint purchase and use a holster when travelling with a firearm-it keeps the gun attached to your person at all times and prevents accidental discharges.

There is an old technique called the "border carry" where you just slide a pistol inside your pants waistband either behind the small of your back or slide around on the side of your hip. This type of carry is certainly very concealable and does not add bulk to your profile, but in terms of security your firearm is only being retained by the pressure of skin against the gun which in turn presses up against the waistband. Walking, running or even sitting down may push the gun around and allow it to slide out of the waistband or fall to the ground. Border carry may be quick and even semi-comfortable, but it does not provide much security for you or your gun.

A regular holster that is fitted to your exact gun can be secured to your person in a number of ways, and will insure the gun does not fall loose. It should also cover the trigger guard of the gun so nothing foreign can be inserted to touch the trigger while it is holstered.

With concealed carry, people often gravitate to the smallest pistols they can find, believing they are easy to carry and more likely to be with them more often than a larger pistol- the smallest of these guns are often referred to as "pocket pistols".

Snub nosed revolvers and small .380 type pistols have often been treated this way. They have long heavy pound trigger pulls which are pretty safe on their own, but are not designed or anticipated to be left floating in a pocket uncovered. Placing a small loaded pistol inside a pants pocket, jacket pocket or purse is once again not a very safe way to secure a firearm. There is nothing to cover the trigger guard and other items in the pocket or purse may get jammed into the trigger and cause an unintended discharge.

Holster manufacturers now make thin holsters which cover the gun and trigger guard and are actually designed to then be inserted whole into a pocket or purse. These pocket holsters are usually semi-sticky and friction drag against surrounding cloth holds it in place. If you have to draw the gun out of the pocket holster friction on the outside of the holster holds it still while the gun is withdrawn. This type of holster is very reasonably priced, adds very little bulk to a small gun, and increases safety and safe carry by a great deal.

When carrying a concealed firearm you must maintain control over the gun at all times, and a holster with a covering strap or locking device is highly recommended. Having someone see a poorly concealed firearm on your person is bad—having your pistol drop out of a cheap open topped holster onto the ground in public is worse. It is potentially dangerous, very embarrassing, and bystanders may call the police and not care whether the gun owner has a Concealed Carry License or what their intentions are.

A quality holster, molded to your exact gun model, which has retention devices built in will prevent your gun from falling off of your person unintentionally, and will also serve to retain it safely on your person in the event of struggle or violent action like a car crash.

When travelling in a vehicle, your concealed carry should either be on your person in a holster, or unloaded and cased. There is no in between state for vehicle carry. It is never safe or tactically advantageous to stuff a gun under the seat, between the seat cushions or even in the glove box. You lose the ability to control the weapon and keep it safe from children, other passengers or even thieves in the event it is forgotten or left unattended.

Citizens without a concealed carry license in most states may only transport a weapon in a vehicle if it is unloaded and secured in some type of case and no ammunition is stored with the gun which would contribute to a rapid access and loading. Storing a weapon separate from the ammunition is still the safest way to keep a weapon in the home or in a vehicle.

Small pistol sized zip up soft padded cases can be obtained for $20 or less and plastic or metal boxes can also be obtained for a small cost. The same safety rules apply to carrying these cases though as apply for the weapon above—do not leave them under the seat, stuffed between the cushions or in the glove box. Imagine yourself as a police officer going to an accident scene or stopping someone for speeding and seeing a gun case in plain view and the driver says "Don't worry, it is not loaded". It is definitely a cause from worry.

Many search and seizure laws developed and interpreted with the state and federal courts to include the U.S. Supreme Court have looked at the lunge area or wing area where a driver could still grab a gun while seated behind the wheel. This area is seen by law enforcement as a potentially dangerous area. If you are transporting an unloaded and cased or secured pistol, it is best to put it in the rear or trunk area as far from the driver as possible.

TRIGGER LOCKS

Trigger locks come in a number of different variations with the goal of making the trigger area inaccessible when the gun is being stored. Some of the oldest trigger locks are a two piece lock which slide onto either side of the trigger guard, clamp together to cover the guard and trigger and then lock into place. They are locked with a key and are very inexpensive running $5 to $10. You will have to evaluate whether you are using the lock on a loaded weapon or an unloaded weapon as part of your firearm safety plan.

Care must be taken with these types of locks because weapons can be stored loaded with the trigger lock affixed. Before depending on them to be a valid safety device for your gun, first try locking it onto the gun while the weapon is unloaded. Then you should tug on the lock back and forth to see if it could be loosened enough to actually engage the trigger and cause the weapon to fire while still locked in place.

Another type of inexpensive lock is the cable type lock. It consists of a keyed padlock which has an armored or aircraft wire cable instead of a normal metal padlock hasp. This type of lock is supplied by many gun manufacturers along with their new guns, and is a very secure locking system. No matter what type of gun it is deployed with, the action or cylinder of the gun must be opened and the cable inserted through the gun and blocking the action open, so it absolutely cannot be fired accidentally. Revolvers could ostensibly be locked open, have rounds stored in the cylinders and cable around the back strap, but semi-automatic pistols must have the magazine removed and the cable run down through the action and magazine well. They range in price from free to about $15 and some are manufactured by well-known brands like Masterlock.

SAFES

Manufacturers make metal pistol "safes" running from book sized boxes to armored cabinets weighing hundreds of pounds. They may have key locks, rotary dial combination locks, finger pressed button combination locks and even fingerprint scanner locks. They may run from $30 to thousands of dollars. Placing a gun in a safe is obviously upgrading your security plan, and if you insist on storing a loaded weapon in your home or vehicle a metal safe is recommended.

Many gun owners wish they could afford the very high dollar and very secure cabinet type safes made by Cannon, Liberty and Browning but don't have the budget or space for them. There are a number of manufacturers on the market like Homak, Stack-on and On-Technology who make light weight stand up safes large enough for several shotguns or rifles for $75-$300. They do not provide the level of security and fire resistance of the much larger safes, but they do provide a significant level of security to a gun owner who needs to keep his firearms out of the reach of children or casual visitors.

These lighter weight safes usually have keyed cylinder locks and would require significant effort and tools by burglars to penetrate. They are similar in size and weight to filing cabinets and would be man portable by one or two burglars-but the addition of guns, ammunition and/or weights can make them too unwieldy to carry. They may also be bolted to studs in the wall for additional security.

Homak and Stack-on make smaller pistol sized cabinet safes of similar materials and lock works which can hold multiple pistols. They are about 8 inches high and about 18-20 inches in length. They are small enough to fit under beds, inside night stands and on closet shelves. They come predrilled with mounting holes and may be bolted or screwed into wall studs. Prices run from $50 to $150.

Another type of budget safe are the small home security safes made by Sentry, Masterlock and Honeywell sold in hardware and home improvement stores for storage of documents, money and valuables. They are small enough to fit in night stands and closets. They have a variety of locks to include rotary dial, push button combinations, keyed locks and even fingerprint readers. They run from $50-$200 depending on size and features. They may have limited tamper and fire protection, and they are easily portable, so they should be bolted or screwed down to prevent carry away theft. Some home office or budget retail stores may offer these type of fire safe or small security safes for even less than $50.

One of the handiest safes for travelling are made by companies like Gunvault which makes the Nano Vault safe. Nano Vault is a metal black box about the size of a hardback book, weighing about 2 lbs, and are just large enough to contain a single pistol and spare magazine or ammo. The safes have either a round cylinder keyed lock, a combination lock or even combination finger keyed pad locks. The versatility is increased with an included cable of aircraft braided steel which can be looped around a seat post, trunk rail in a vehicle, a bed rail or plumbing pipe or other non-moving items at home or in a hotel.

Can these items be defeated? Of course, with enough time and enough tools, they can be removed and taken away and opened like any other safe, but they will prevent the casual removal or exposure of firearms while travelling or at home. Gun carriers may not have anticipated having to store their gun in a hotel or vehicle, so these small safes fill a very active necessity on the road. The prices run from about $25-$60 depending on features.

ILLINOIS SAFETY LAW RELATED TO CHILD PROTECTION AND GUN STORAGE

Under 720 ILCS 5/24-9, it is illegal for anyone to store or leave a firearm in a premises they control where they have reason to believe a minor under the age to 14 years would be likely to have access or gain access to the gun without parental control and the minor causes death or great bodily harm with the firearm. The gun owner would be prosecuted under a Class C misdemeanor unless the gun is:

(1) Secured with a device or mechanism (other than the firearm safety) designed to make a firearm inoperable.
(2) Secured in a lock box or container
(3) Kept in a location where a "reasonable person" would believe the firearm would be secure from a minor under the age of 14 gaining access

The law also states under 24-9 (c) the gun owner/handler would not be held accountable if the minor under 14 uses the gun in a lawful act of self-defense, or if the minor made unlawful entry to the premises where the gun was stored.

http://codes.lp.findlaw.com/ilstatutes/720/5/24/24-9#sthash.qJ8IKkFe.dpuf.

113

CHAPTER ELEVEN
DEALING WITH LAW ENFORCEMENT.

By law, if an Illinois resident meets a Police Officer in the conduct of his official duties, must the legally armed citizen immediately inform the Police Officer they are carrying a legally concealed weapon and in possession of a valid Illinois Concealed Carry License?

No. Under the Illinois Firearm Concealed Carry Act 430 ILCS 66/10(g)-(h), a license or License holder is NOT required under the Illinois law to immediately inform an officer they have a legally concealed firearm on their person. Some states make this a mandatory disclosure, and with Illinois' very strict rules about concealed carry it is surprising they did not require armed citizens to announce their condition. But it is not mandated by Illinois law.

However, under 430 ILCS 66/10(h), if an officer and citizen are in an "investigative stop" initiated by the officer, (traffic stop, questioning on the street or at a building etc), and the officer asks the Concealed Carry License holder if they are in possession of a firearm-then the Illinois law mandates the citizen MUST disclose they have a legally concealed firearm on their person and provide the License upon request of the officer along with the identity and location of the firearm.

If you are carrying concealed, ALWAYS have your License and FOID with you-failure to do so may result in your arrest for carrying an illegally concealed weapon. (Think of it as always carrying your driver's license when you drive. Even though you are fully licensed by the state and it can be looked up via computer, if you are caught driving without your license you can be cited.)

NEVER touch, handle or present the firearm in the presence of the law officer unless specifically directed to do so. If asked to provide the Concealed Weapon License, do so only when asked by the officer, inform them of the location of the License (pocket, wallet, purse etc) and verbally advise when you are going to retrieve the License. There should be no surprises, and any movement should be predicated with a verbal announcement of intention, and no sudden movements or attempts to leave or run will be tolerated.

In a vehicle, if you can access your driver's license and registration that would be a good time to provide your Concealed Carry License as well. However, if the officer is approaching or already at your window, make especially sure to not bend over, reach under the seat or into the glove box for any type of license without first telling the officer that is your intention and what is in that container or area hidden from view.

This same advice is good for any traffic stop. Remain behind the wheel of your car, lower your window and turn off any music so you can speak with the officer and place both hands upon the steering wheel. DO NOT lunge and grab at items in the car like purses or under the seat-this creates a potentially dangerous position for you and may expose a weapon on your person. Retrieve your driver's license upon the officer's request and follow all directions.

In a traffic stop situation, it is preferable (but not mandated) for an armed Concealed Carry License holder who has a legally concealed weapon in the vehicle or on their person, to go ahead and voluntarily disclose to the officer you have a valid Illinois Concealed Carry License and a legally concealed weapon with you. Accompany this with the announcement where your license is kept, where the weapon is located, and you will not make any movement until directed by the officer.

This voluntary disclosure allows the officer the very necessary ability to control the situation for both the citizen and the officer's mutual safety. If the officer makes requests about movement or restraint, follow all directions to insure you do not create a dangerous situation where the officer may feel imperiled. Officers may have daily interaction with the public via traffic stops, but consider the officer's viewpoint where each stop is made with a total stranger and has a potential for injury or violence. Be polite and cooperative during any such contact and the officer will treat you with the respect and professionalism owed to a law abiding citizen.

Imagine yourself in the officer's place during a similar occurrence-they are required to enforce the law and having just met a citizen who acknowledges having a firearm on their person, this will naturally put them on the defensive. They are required to determine whether the citizen is in fact legally in possession of a valid Illinois Concealed Carry License in addition to the firearm. Finding or observing an undisclosed firearm will force any officer to respond with potential use of force to protect their own lives first and they can sort out the legal facts about licenses and legal possession second.

The text of the relevant law is below:

Firearm Concealed Carry Act 430 ILCS 66/10(g)-(h)
(g) A licensee shall possess a license at all times the licensee carries a concealed firearm except:

(h) If an officer of a law enforcement agency initiates an investigative stop, including but not limited to a traffic stop, of a licensee who is carrying a concealed firearm, upon the request of the officer the licensee shall disclose to the officer that he or she is in possession of a concealed firearm under this Act, present the license upon the request of the officer, and identify the location of the concealed firearm.

CHAPTER TWELVE
MARKSMANSHIP.

The Illinois law regarding training for the CCL license mandates trainees get some formal marksmanship training as part of the curriculum, actual gun handling and range time.

Marksmanship is a rather broad concept. While a student cannot become an accomplished Marksman by merely reading about the subject, being lectured on the topic or shooting 30 bullets for a final score, they can learn about the fundamentals of shooting accurately and about the amount of mental preparation and involvement necessary to shoot well. Combining knowledge and mental involvement with physical practice with a firearm are all necessary elements of marksmanship.

The Random House College Dictionary-Revised Edition, Random House Inc, New York 1982, defines "Marksman" as "1. A person skilled in shooting at a mark. 2. U.S. Mil. The lowest rating in rifle marksmanship."

Firearm owners should all possess marksmanship skills, but it is somewhat interesting to see the definition listing marksman as the lowest level of military shooting skill. Expert is of course at the top.

It would be amazing if every CCL License holder was an Expert Marksman, but that unfortunately is not the truth. Many people who own guns have very little experience with them, don't train with them, don't maintain them, and hope in case of emergency the gun will work like some kind of magic wand.

Concealed weapons license holders need to become very familiar with the cycle of operation of their firearm, the loading and unloading process, keeping the weapon safe and concealed, and ultimately being able to shoot the firearm accurately if called upon.

Watching television and movie actors shooting with unerring accuracy and no recoil with bad guys falling instantly incapacitated does not equate to real life any more than using video game controllers to fight entire digital battles equates to a real war.

New shooters often do not appreciate how difficult it is to properly align the sights, press the trigger and absorb the felt recoil to hit a static target even at close ranges. For someone who watched "Dirty Harry" shoot his .44 Magnum pistol with a single hand with no ill effect in the movies, the real world may intrude quite unpleasantly. The simple physics of shooting a gun with the resulting recoil and noise may be daunting at first. Many new shooters start with a large and powerful handgun and encounter difficulties which make them shy away from continued practice.

An offshoot problem, is putting extremely small pistols in the hands of new shooters. Small guns have shorter sighting planes, may have large amounts of recoil with smaller gripping surfaces and are more difficult to shoot well.

Well-meaning husbands talk of getting a small gun for their wife but don't associate a small gun with being more difficult to shoot. It is always a good idea to involve the other person in a selection process to include having them handle and feel the differences in different gun frame sizes and calibers.

Getting instruction from qualified and experienced instructors or shooters is always the best way to learn to shoot well. However, not everyone has that opportunity, and may have to practice on their own and learn by doing.

Even with all of the mechanical and physical actions going on, sheer repetition is not enough to make one a good shooter. **Bad practice only reinforces bad behaviors**. Good shooting involves a very large amount of mental direction and concentration to make all of the aspects work together.

Concealed permit holders absolutely must be competent with their firearms and their decision making abilities in a deadly force encounter-it is no less serious than life and death itself. Col. Jeff Cooper is credited by many as fathering and promoting modern pistol fighting techniques which have been adopted and improved upon by the police, military and civilian shooters. He is credited with saying "Owning a handgun doesn't make you armed any more than owning a guitar makes you a musician." http:www.buckeyfirearmsorg/quotations-jeff cooper.

FUNDAMENTALS OF MARKSMANSHIP
THE SHOOTING STANCE.

This is the platform where marksmanship starts-simply standing on the ground in a stable position. Feet are usually described as being approximately shoulder width apart and facing downrange towards a target. The strong side foot may be slightly back by a matter of a few inches in a comfortable position. Keeping the shoulder's width distance is much more stable than placing your feet close together.

By leaning slightly forward and placing the essential body weight over the balls of the feet and knees slightly bent, you are able to counter balance holding a pistol at arm's length in front of you (it can be heavy!) and also the forward leaning attitude helps soak up recoil easier and more efficiently than merely standing straight up. Do not lock your knees into a rigid position. There should not be any appreciable strain from standing in this shoulder width position for several minutes. It is slightly wider than a "natural stance", but not a lot wider.

Extend the weapon and your arms forward. Again, keep your elbows slightly bent or not locked in place. Holding a firearm in front of your body becomes fatiguing very quickly, and having locked elbows makes it harder to hold the gun out for extended periods. If you become fatigued or have the need to hold a gun in place for an extended time, merely bending your elbows slightly relieves the tension and is a more comfortable and endurable position.

There are several acknowledged techniques for holding a pistol which have developed over time. When black powder pistols were first used in duels they were fired with the strong hand only with the weak hand (or off-hand) placed behind the back, on the hip, or in a pocket. This technique is still used exclusively in Bull's-eye style target shooting and is the epitome of marksmanship. Using one hand to support the weight of the gun at full arm's extension is a difficult way to accurately shoot a gun. Mastery of this position requires much practice and concentration.

However, every shooter should have some practice shooting with the strong hand unsupported and with the weak hand unsupported in case they are ever in a situation where they cannot place two hands on the gun or one hand is injured.

This single hand hold shooting remained part of American hand gunning through the implementation of more effective and multi-shot pistols and continued through the Revolutionary War and, the pioneer and Wild West days.

Our ideas of an old west fast draw gunfight always involved the single handed draw and firing of a pistol from a holster-and oft times involved fanning the hammer with the offhand to re-cock and fire the pistol rapidly. But these images come to us from television and the movies-not from reality. There were very few instances in the west of stand in the street at high noon fast draw gunfights, and fanning a gun for rapid shots was almost unheard of and terrible waste of ammunition.

Both Wild Bill Hickok and Wyatt Earp are credited in American history as being pistoleers or gunfighters. Study of their few actual shootings found they both used one hand to draw and fire the gun and took the time to aim.

Bill Hickok may have been one of the most accurate and revered gunfighters of the day, and it was said he was not blazingly fast, but he was very deliberate and hit what he aimed at. Good tactics for the modern day.

In 1865, Hickok was actually involved in one of the very few TV style duels in the street. The distance was reputed to be 75 yards apart and Hickok steadied his pistol across his opposite arm. Both parties fired at the same time and Hickok's fatal bullet struck home.

Quite interestingly, studies of modern police and armed citizen "gun fights" have established an average distance for an American shooting to be 21 feet or less, or seven yards. As a result of those studies a lot of modern firearm training places heavy emphasis on these close distances or Close Quarter Battle scenarios. Most experienced shooters would be hard pressed to make a 75 yard shot on a man sized target ala Hickok.

Single handed pistol shooting continued to be trained through World Wars I and II. In World War II, some variation was taught adding a squatting position to the stance. The feet were held wider than shoulder stance and center of gravity lowered significantly into a semi-squatting position with the gun held in the strong hand pointed towards the target.

Benefits of this stance were added stability from the lowered center of gravity, and the shooter had reduced their own silhouette or made them a smaller target. Detriments included being very difficult to move quickly from this semi-squat.

Police adopted this technique and used it in the 1940's and 1950's and it can still be seen in figurines atop shooting trophies patterned after the technique.

Another variation evolved in that time frame where the non-shooting arm was bent into a V-shape and held tightly against the chest area to shield the heart and lung area.

It was not until the late 1950's and early 1960's when the idea of holding a gun in both hands came into vogue with police and competition shooters. It was developed by "Combat Shooters" like Jeff Cooper who brought tactics, speed and accuracy together in more efficient and accurate techniques which were augmented by the stability afforded by a two handed hold on the pistol grip. Law enforcement started implementing these more advanced techniques and two handed shooting with feet shoulder width apart and knees slightly bent remains the most popular form of shooting being taught today.

Making a naturally pointing V or "isosceles triangle" using both hands and arms is the easiest position to learn and practice. It is much more comfortable than single handed shooting and easier to maintain over longer periods of time. The triangle position is also inherently a very strong position with support from arm, shoulder and back muscles.

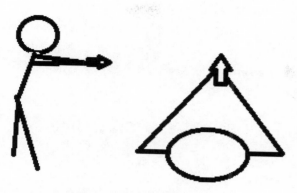

Isoscelese Triangle Stance

Another competition inspired stance evolved from a Los Angeles County Sheriff's Deputy named Jack Weaver who was also a competition shooter. In the "Weaver Stance" the arms assume a push/pull position with the gun hand extended forward and the offhand gripping the pistol and pulling back and the weak side elbow is bent significantly. Weaver was a very successful competition shooter and this technique quickly spread throughout the competition ranks and into law enforcement training. It is certainly a viable shooting stance, but takes more training to learn than the natural V position.

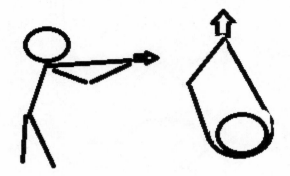

Weave Stance-support hand bent elbow

American law enforcement has gone back to teaching the V shaped position instead of the Weaver stance. Part of this change may be connected to the more "natural" pointing position pushing both hands towards the target in a V position.

The other identified part of the law enforcement change is the now routine use of body armor. With the V stance, the broadest facing of the body armor faces the target. With the Weaver stance, the torso is twisted slightly and can expose the side/armpit area of the body which has less armor coverage.

Is the V stance better than the Weaver stance? Is the Weaver superior to the V stance? Not necessarily, but using an Isosceles V does take into account the body's natural affinity to shove/deflect or point at a danger. The non-gun holding hand can also be released easily into a deflection or defensive extended posture and the gun hand pulled back towards the body to prevent entanglement or gun take-away.

Through repetition, the Weaver stance or other variants can be learned and made the go-to response, but in an emergency the unconscious response to dangers are going to take over no matter where feet are planted, how shoulders are aligned or whatever the current "correct" posture is supposed to be.

GRIP AND DRAW

This seems like a simple topic-just grab the gun and pull it out! Like anything else in life, there are some fundamental issues which will help get it right, and repetition will cement the practice in place.

The simplest concept with "Grip and Draw" is when you initially place a hand on the gun's grip; understand that is your final grip.

That initial grab is the best grip you are ever going to have time to establish. There is no time to readjust, wiggle or jiggle the grip into a better or more comfortable position. An imperfect grip must be ignored during draw/fire iterations in favor of other tactical and marksmanship concepts involved with aligning the sights and pulling the trigger smoothly.

When you grip and draw a weapon, it needs to be done quickly and smoothly, moving the gun from its concealed position into a muzzle forward movement facing the target with simple economy of motion. With this in mind, pay attention in training and practice to establishing a firm grip well seated in the web of the hand while in the holster.

Semi-automatic pistol grips and even revolver grips have many different shapes which may or may not fit the ergonomics of the shooter's hand. One size does not fit all well or comfortably. It is important to put as much of your palm and supporting fingers onto the handgrip. Establish your grip with the web of your hand as high up on the semi-automatic pistol handgrip or back strap as you can.

Some add on grips or molded grips may have finger ridges on them. In a quick grab and draw, your fingers may end up on top of the ridges instead of in the valleys-but that is the grip you have for the moment and you need to make the shot regardless of the less than great position of the gun in your palm.

Small pistols may have a very limited surface area and you may only get two support fingers wrapped around the butt. Grabbing the gun with web of your hand as high as you can get it will help lessen the problems of not having all of your support fingers on the gun. (Some add on floor plates have an extra ledge for an additional finger to hold on to. These plates are very cheap and easy to install and add an impressive degree of controllability over a small gun without a pinkie grip. Pearce Grip is one of the originators of these add on products.)

Revolver Grip.

Revolvers have very curved handgrips which may or may not fit well into the palm of your gripping/drawing hand. For many years production revolver grips seemed to come in two sizes-too big or too small.

Large production revolvers often come from the factory with stated "oversized" grips which fit most human beings poorly. They were thick wooden grips that flared at the base where we actually need a tapered area to facilitate a two handed grip. Conversely, small snub nosed types of revolvers often come from the factory with minimal curved handle grips which are good for concealment but also difficult to hold on to, especially with strong recoiling ammunition.

Shooters should evaluate their ability to grip a pistol or revolver securely, and if necessary replace any ill-fitting grips with after-market grips which fit their hand better.

Hogue and other manufacturers provide a myriad of replacement grips, styles and materials. Replacing the tiny grips on a small revolver with rubber molded Hogue grips will do wonders for the ability to hold, grip and shoot the gun comfortably and accurately.

Draw.

After establishing a good grip and releasing any safety devices on the holster, the gun may now be drawn from the holster in a smooth movement. Some holsters internal friction resists the removal and the gun needs to be tugged smartly instead of being drug out slowly.

The muzzle of the gun is tilted upwards until it is parallel with the floor and then extended forward. Once it has cleared the holster and pointed toward the target it can be fired one handed at very close combat distances.

The goal is not an old time TV cowboy "quick draw." The goal is a smooth draw of the gun and aligning it with the target with a minimum of extra movement.

Try yanking an empty gun out of a holster as hard as possible and shoving it towards the target. When the gun reaches full extension you will see an enormous amount of additional movement with the gun and hands bouncing from the forces involved with the thrust. It will take additional seconds before the gun can come to rest and the sights can be aligned. While it is "as fast as possible" it is much slower than using a smooth draw.

Smooth is fast.

Drawing a pistol out smoothly, meeting the off hand at the centerline of the body, adding the offhand to the grip and pushing forwarded to full extension results in little to no wobble and the gun and sights are already nearly aligned when the arms meet full extension.

Adding a stopwatch or digital timer to a smooth draw and fire technique vs a "fast as possible" draw and fire will graphically demonstrate the time difference. If you are developing good shooting habits and marksmanship skills, saving one second or even half seconds with a smooth draw and accurate shot may be the difference in life and death.

Digital shooting timers are very valuable tools for the developing shooter. They not only provide a start beep, but they measure the time until the first shot and each follow up shot in thousandths of a second. Choppy trigger work or sloppy draw/fire will be easily revealed on the timer.

Dedicated hand held competition timers are available for around $100-$150. Several shot timer smartphone apps are available for I-phones and Android phones for free or for very small fees. If you don't have a coach or experienced instructor to mentor your developing marksmanship a digital timer can be of considerable assistance in teaching yourself.

The second half of the grip sequence involves adding your weak hand (or off hand) to the gun after it is drawn from the holster, but before it is on target. It is very important to not point the muzzle of the gun at your off hand before it is added to the grip! (Lasering- Safety Rule #3 **Never point a gun at anything you are not willing to shoot or destroy-** and Safety Rule #2 **Keep your finger off the trigger until you are ready to shoot!**).

Slow practice is necessary to develop good form. Stage your left hand with palm open near the centerline or solar plexus of your body. Establish a grip while in the holster, draw the weapon out and move it towards the target. Meet the gun with your empty week hand and add the gripping surface of the palm and fingers around the gun.

If you hold a gun in your strong hand you will notice a large area of the weak side grip is exposed-this area should be met and filled with the meaty part under the thumb of your empty weak hand. Once that pad lands in the empty portion of the handgrip, wrap your fingers around the front of the grip on top of your strong hand fingers. This is your final grip. Again, there will be no time to adjust the grip during a draw and fire sequence, so practice this slowly and smoothly to maintain a uniform presentation and grip.

The pistol is brought up to eye level in the two handed grip and arms extended. Avoid bringing your head down to the gun. A straight push from center line to eye level is an economical motion and does not infer stress or body movement in the neck and torso.

Grip Strength.

How tight should you grip the gun? The resulting two handed grip should simulate a strong handshake. It is impossible to shoot a pistol well or manage recoil with a loose grip. The weak hand should provide 70% of the amount of wrapping/compressing force exerted upon the grip with the strong hand providing 30%. The reason for this unbalanced exertion lies in the problem which results when you exert gripping strength (a gross motor skill). Combining a gross motor skill like grip with a fine motor skill like pulling a trigger with a single finger causes conflicting and jerky movements in the hands. It is very

difficult to grip with both hands with
still expect a single trigger finger to b
or smoothly.

This bit of ergonomic conflict is easil
make a tightly clenched fist with an e
fist held very tight manipulate your in
finger- you will feel the resulting amo
jerkiness in your index finger while y
keep a tightly clenched fist.

Repeat the sequence with a normal or
and the index finger moves easily and
only 30% grip strength in your gun h
with the gun but also retain the ability
finger freely. The 70% wrap with the
solid two hand grip is maintained.

With a semi-automatic pistol in a two
thumbs will lie along the left side of
you have established the grip by inse
of the weak hand onto the open hand
side thumb should then rest on your :
and your strong hand thumb will lie

It is important with a semi-auto pisto
weak hand thumb over the top of yo
and let it lie across the web of your s
weak side thumb is laid over the top
weak thumb will rest behind the pist
right side of the gun grip. When firir
the slide will recoil during the ejecti

trong pressure and
able to move freely

observed if you
npty hand. With the
dex finger as a trigger
unt of tension and
ou are still trying to

lightly clenched fist
smoothly. By using
nd you retain contact
to move your trigger
weak hand insures a

handed grip, your
he pistol receiver. If
ting the palm/thumb
grip area, your weak
ndex finger/knuckle
top your weak thumb.

to not cross your
r weak hand thumb
rong hand. If your
n this manner, your
l slide and onto the
g a gun in this manner,
n sequence and may

The same applies to the target. If the target is in perfect focus you are not focused on your sights. It is ok for the target to be a bit fuzzy or indistinct while you focus instead on your sights.

The front sight is centered square with the rear sight placed at the base of the target, and the top of the front sight is centered from side to side within the rear sight with equal space on both sides of the front sight.

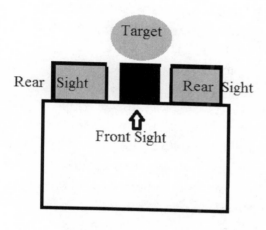

If the front sight is higher than the tops of the rear sight, the bullet will impact higher than intended. The same applies to bullets which strike low because the front sight is lower than the rear sights. If the front sight is pushed unevenly to the right or left side inside the rear sights the resulting bullet impact will follow the front sight.

Once you align the sights properly, you will quickly notice they are floating and moving around often in a figure 8. Your muscles, ligaments, breathing and even your heartbeat will constantly cause motion in a pointed weapon. This is normal and with more practice you will experience less movement.

If you could press the trigger perfectly while the sights are aligned and pointed at the target with no other movement the bullet would fly unerringly to target. However, it is impossible to halt all extraneous movement in the human body. You must practice and concentrate on good form to become an accurate and consistent shooter.

Eye Focus.

You can shoot with both eyes open, or with one eye shut. Traditionally we learn to close the weak side eye and focus with the strong side eye on sight alignment. One of the negative aspects is the loss of peripheral vision. If you learn to shoot with both eyes open you will see a much larger field of view-an important aspect of concealed carry and close combat distance shooting. You may have to keep track of your family members and members of the public in addition to the suspect(s) so both eyes open is a good thing.

. It takes quite a bit of focused practice to learn to shoot with both eyes open and still see the front sight align correctly, but your controlling or dominant eye should assume most of the work. Both eyes open works well out to about 15 yards and most people have to close one eye at longer distances.

Eye Dominance.

Most people have their strong side hand match their dominant eye and don't have any problems with sights. Some people are cross eye dominant,-the eye on the opposite side from their strong hand has dominance.

A simple way to find out which eye is your strong eye, is to make an "OK" sign with fingers of both hands. Stack the two circles on top of each other and extend your arms to full length. Look through the circles and move it quickly to your face arriving at your dominant eye.

You can do a separate test by holding an index finger up while extended at arm's length. Look at the finger and beyond. Close your right eye and then your left eye. You will notice the image does not change much with your dominant eye open. The image changes or seems to jump in the opposite direction with the non-dominant eye.

If you have a cross eye dominance you can compensate with several different pistol techniques. Shooting with both eyes open may help. You can try to learn to close your dominant eye but it does not feel as comfortable as having the dominant eye open.

You can also use a modified bent elbow or Weaver type stance to line up the sights in front of your dominant eye. You can also try cocking your head at an angle to more closely align your dominant eye or canting the pistol about 45% over toward the dominant eye instead of holding the pistol in a vertical hold.

You can even teach yourself to shoot the pistol with your weak hand to take advantage of your dominant eye on that side. Cross eye dominance can be frustrating, but early recognition of the dominance and training to compensate can overcome this feature.

Point Shooting.

If you read much about modern gun fighting techniques you will find much mention and many advocates of "point shooting" in close combat situations. This entails shoving the pistol forward with either two hands or single handed and engaging the trigger rapidly without aligning the sights.

Another variation is bringing the pistol to face level and using the entire pistol as the aiming device without using actual sight alignment. This technique takes advantage of very close targets and a natural instinct to be able to point towards a target without making sight references.

With practice, this technique can be very quick and surprisingly accurate. The point shooting concepts were developed at the turn of the century and between the world wars by British soldiers and policemen Capt William Fairbairn and Capt Eric Sykes. They are well known as developing the Sykes/Fairbairn Commando knife used during WWII. They also taught gun fighting, knife fighting and empty handed fighting to Singapore Police and Allied troops.

American Colonel Rex Applegate learned these techniques from Sykes and Fairbairn during WWII and passed them along to the OSS and American special operators during WWII. A number of American combat shooting schools still teach point shooting as a viable technique.

Breathing.

People breathe all day long without noticing and may not notice while shooting there is a natural pause while aligning the sights and before breaking a shot. Shooters often hold their breath hoping it will steady the movement of the gun and end up exerting additional stress and feeling exaggerated movement and oxygen deprivation!

Breathe normally and accept the gun will move minimally no matter what you do and your body will stop breathing briefly during most shots. With a slight exhale there will be a small pause at the end where your body feels more at rest and there may be less tension exerted on the gun.

Trigger control.

Again, combined with alignment of the sights, the trigger pull or trigger press are the keys to marksmanship. Do not yank or jerk the trigger. Do not clench your entire trigger finger hand. These movements will drag or torque the entire pistol to the side. This is a small movement but it is exaggerated over distance and a small movement at the firing line can result in missing the entire target at 15 or 25 yards.

There are several different trigger/action types mentioned in the Safety section and they vary mechanically, but the advice to press the trigger remains constant. Press with steady and even pressure. This should not move the sights out of alignment

When you decide to start pressing the trigger, move it to completion and do not stop or hesitate. Anticipating the explosion or flinching in expectation of the detonation will jerk the pistol off target.

Commit to the trigger pull. Do not try and guess the precise moment the gun will fire, this will result in more anticipation movement. The goal is a "surprise shot" with the gun firing while you are still committed to deliberate trigger pressure while the sights remain aligned.

Once the gun fires reset or release the trigger forward to ready the gun to fire again. With practice you can determine the exact amount of release needed to ready the weapon-it may not need to be released all the way out depending on the weapon.

Keep your finger on the trigger through the entire cycle, and if you are not going to shoot again immediately take your finger off the trigger and place it alongside the frame and outside of the trigger guard.

Follow through.

As the hammer falls and causes the cartridge in the chamber to fire, continue the trigger press and follow the recoil. Reacquire the front sight and then the sight picture as the pistol comes out of recoil. Pressure on the trigger is released so it can move forward and reset and engage the internal safeties or lock works. The finger releases the trigger back forward but should remain on the trigger and prepare for a second or follow up shot. Failure to exert follow through is most often noticed with scattered target groupings. Making a shot and immediately working to line up for a second shot is all part of follow through.

Committing to the series of actions necessary to make the next shot will help insure smooth sequence and accuracy. Draw, align the sights and press on the trigger, ride the recoil, allow the trigger to reset and require the sights. Follow through insures all of the acts are smooth and not jerky.

The final piece of follow-through advice is if you are finished shooting, you still must be mindful of the security and safety of your weapon. If you are going to holster the weapon keep your finger outside the trigger guard and visually check to insure the hammer is not cocked. Insure any external safety is in the ON position. Some shooters holster their weapon with their thumb on top of the hammer as another physical check of the condition of the hammer and slide. This will help the shooter feel sure the hammer is down or decocked, and the slide is locked forward in battery.

When placing the gun into the holster, always tuck the muzzle in first before making any other adjustments. Some holsters do not stay open completely or may need additional attention to get the gun seated. Shooters often reach over with their non-shooting hand to help settle the gun in the holster and end up lasering their off- hand in the process.

If you need help getting the gun settled, be sure to first put the muzzle into the leading edge of the holster and do not wave it across your support hand or lower your support hand below the muzzle of the gun. Only after the gun is secured back in the holster can you mentally relax.

Mental process.

There is a lot of thinking that goes on in good shooting. There are a lot of small actions described above just in the firing sequence. Thinking your way through it is a necessary part of marksmanship and skill building. If you decide to shoot two times, then mentally commit to all of the actions necessary to align the sights, press the trigger and reset ahead of time and stay concentrated on process.

New shooters are often told to repeat "Front sight. Front sight. Front sight." as they are learning to draw the gun and align the sights before pressing the trigger. Another similar mantra is "Trigger and sights. Trigger and sights." used to mentally talk your way through getting the trigger started, checking sight alignment and double checking the trigger press continues without disturbing the sight alignment.

If you seem to be flinching and anticipating the loud bang and recoil try self-correcting with a repeated mantra to focus on the trigger press and sight alignment instead.

DRY FIRE EXERCISE-UNLOADED WEAPON

Insure the weapon is unloaded. Remove all ammunition from the area. Inspect the chamber, cylinders or magazine well to insure no ammunition is present in the firearm.

Locate a safe direction to point the weapon. This drill can help insure or correct sight alignment and consistent trigger press as well as smooth operation. Holding the weapon parallel to the floor, balance a dime on a flat side across the front sight. Raise the gun slowly to eye level without disturbing the dime. Align the sights of the unloaded weapon on a safe area or target (TREAT EVERY GUN AS IF IT IS LOADED) and press the trigger smoothly. The trigger pull should not disturb the dime on the front sight.

Revolver hammers may have a longer travel distance and with more energy imparted to the frame of the gun the hammer fall may knock the dime off the front sight. However the point of the dime technique is to insure the sights are aligned and triggers are moved smoothly and the dime is not disturbed before the hammer strikes.

Another variation of this drill for semi-automatic pistols is to use an empty brass cartridge instead of the dime and just balance the base of the cartridge on top of the square slide just behind the front sight.

Modern firearms should not be damaged by dry fire exercises. If you have any concerns about it contact the manufacturer of your firearm for advice or obtain items which are made to cushion the blow of the firing pin or striker.

There are products known as "Snap Caps" and other brand names which look like cartridges made of brightly colored plastic but are completely safe and inert and are placed into the chamber of guns to simulate cycling yet cushion the blow of the hammer/firing pin during dry firing. You can make similar items by driving the primers out of some empty brass and gluing a piece of pencil eraser into the empty flash hole/primer pocket.

CHAPTER THIRTEEN
CLEANING, LOADING AND UNLOADING.

The Illinois law regarding training for the CCL license mandates cleaning, loading and unloading of firearms training.

Loading and unloading of pistols and revolvers was mentioned in the Safety section, but will addressed here again to insure the process is fully covered.

Revolver loading.

Revolver loading starts with pointing the weapon in a safe direction.

Hold the revolver by the hand grip in the strong-hand with finger outside the trigger guard. Reach under the middle of the weapon with the weak-hand palm up. With the weak hand thumb or strong hand thumb engage the cylinder release and push the cylinder through the left side of the frame with the fingers of the weak hand. Grasp the cylinder and gun immediately with the weak hand with the fingers through the frame with fingers wrapped around the cylinder and remove the strong hand from the gun. Now holding the revolver with the opened cylinder entirely in the weak hand, tip the barrel towards the floor or as near to straight down as possible. Holding the weapon close to the belt line will facilitate this position. You may now insert loaded cartridges in to the open cylinder holes with the strong hand.

When finished loading resume a strong hand grip on the butt of the gun and push the cylinder closed into the frame with the weak hand. Revolve the cylinder slightly until it engages and is locked into place

Revolver unload.

To unload a revolver, open the cylinder as described above and while held in the weak hand with fingers through the frame and around the cylinder tip the muzzle straight up. Use the flat of the strong hand to compress the ejector rod one time to full compression (spring loaded metal rod extending in front of the cylinder). The empty or full cartridges should fall directly to the floor. Turn the revolver back over with muzzle down to resume loading sequence.

Loading and unloading a revolver it is important to use straight up and down positions. Any efforts to load or unload the gun while it is horizontal to the floor make the process more difficult and may actually trap brass under the ejector rod assembly.

Revolver drop in reloaders are available which are much quicker than loading single rounds. These reloaders hold rounds already aligned for the empty cylinder holes. You slide or drop the loader into the empty chambers, twist or depress a retaining knob and the bullets drop into the cylinder and you set the reloader aside.

One of the original products was called the "Six Second Speed Loader". This was a vast improvement over other old reload techniques for revolvers, but is substantially slower than a semi-automatic pistol being reloaded in one second or less with a magazine.

Other revolver loader alternatives include "Speed Strips" by Bianchi which are a short rubber strip that holds six rounds side by side by their bases. It can be used to load one or two rounds at a time into an empty cylinder.

A long time product which still works are small "dump pouches" that snap over belts hold six rounds either all together or with two rounds held tightly in three pockets.

During a reload, the pouch is unsnapped and rounds are "dumped" into the palm of the empty hand or grasped and loaded two at a time. If this pouch is worn on the belt it is worn on the strong side near the belt buckle or appendix, as the weapon will be suspended in the weak hand during loading and unloading and the strong hand will do the actual loading.

Semi-Auto load.

Loading a semi-automatic pistol simply involves inserting a loaded magazine into the butt of the weapon and cycling the slide.

If the gun has external safeties place them in the ON position. Hold the gun in the strong hand, pointed in a safe direction and finger off the trigger. The slide may be locked to the rear or fully forward. Insert the magazine until is clicks into place.

It is good to tap the bottom of the magazine or tug on it to insure it is locked into place. To finish the loading sequence, if the slide is locked to the rear tug the slide backwards and let it snap home or slingshot into place.

Another method is to depress the slide stop which is holding the slide open. Semi-autos are manufactured to load via the full spring compression, so the slingshot technique is preferred.

Do not ease or ride the slide home or cushion it in an effort to be less harsh with the gun.

If you inserted the magazine into a pistol with the slide closed, grasp the rear of the slide between the thumb and forefinger of the weak hand and pull the slide fully back and let it slingshot forward.

Semi auto unload.

To unload semi-automatic pistols first engage any external safeties. With finger out of the trigger guard and the gun held in the strong hand, remove the magazine. **A loaded round may remain in the chamber so the slide must be cycled at least once to eject the round.** The slide may be locked open by pulling it to the rear by the weak hand and engaging the slide stop with the thumb of the strong hand into the slide lock notch cut-out on the bottom of the slide.

When you have unloaded the pistol, slingshot the slide to full extension several times then lock it to the rear to insure any round in the chamber ejects from the gun. Cycling the slide several times helps in case the extractor has gotten dirty and does not grip the rim of the shell casing in the chamber/barrel. Once completed, visually and physically inspect the chamber and the magazine well to insure no cartridges or magazine remains in the weapon and it is truly unloaded and rendered safe.

If a magazine pouch is worn on the belt it should be worn on the weak side on the hip or slightly in front of the hip with the bullets pointed forward or centerline.

The unloaded weapon is retained in the strong hand and the weak hand pulls the fresh magazine out of the pouch using the thumb and middle finger. The index finger lies down along the spine of the magazine. As the magazine is turned upright the index finger helps angle the device into the magazine well of the pistol in a "hand finds hand" maneuver. With practice, the unloading and reloading of a semi-auto pistol can easily be managed into one to two seconds.

Ideally, when reloading a semi-automatic pistol the gun is brought in fairly close to the chest/face before loading instead of leaving it out at full arm's extension.

By bringing it closer to the body it allows the shooter to still look down range for potential danger while still having the gun in their main center of vision. This position is quick to load to and the shooter does not have to look up and down to visually orient on the gun while assessing down range activity.

Press Check.

There is a technique known as "Press Check" which allows a weapon handler to visually insure a semi-automatic pistol is loaded (Safety Rule #1 **ALWAYS TREAT EVERY GUN AS IF IT IS LOADED**). You can Press Check without having to disassemble the weapon or unload it completely.

Press Check allows the handler to retract the slide a small amount, visually confirm the presence of a cartridge in the chamber, and return the slide forward back into battery.

Note: If the handler retracts the slide fully, any loaded round will be extracted from the chamber and ejected from the weapon.

You cannot Press Check a revolver-just open the cylinder inspect the loaded cartridges-DO NOT tip a revolver up and count the tips or front of the visible bullets in an effort to see if the gun is loaded (**ALWAYS POINT A GUN IN A SAFE DIRECTION**/ Safety Rule #3 **NEVER POINT A GUN AT ANYTHING YOU ARE NOT WILLING TO SHOOT OR DESTROY**).

It is always a good idea to insure your pistol is still loaded after you have seen it last.

Some guns have a visual or physical "loaded chamber indicator" which is a small tab which extends out of the slide when there is a round in the chamber. See your owner's manual to see if this type of device is present on your gun. Even with a loaded chamber indicator, you may still want to double check to see the gun is loaded and in a condition which would allow it to fire.

To Press Check a semi-auto, first point the weapon in a safe direction. Place the weapon in the strong-hand with the thumb and web under the tang or shelf which is under the hammer, your fingers lie across the top of the slide, and the muzzle protrudes past the bottom of your palm. NOTE: No fingers are anywhere near the trigger or the muzzle. Your fingers lie between the breech and rear sight-do not get your fingers caught or pin

Press Check. Depending (

have two, three or all fou

sights and the breech.

By squeezing your finger

each other this will cause

amount. A quarter of an

sufficient to open the bre

portion of a brass or nicl

without ejecting the rou

Releasing the strength ir

You may then replace

insert the magazin

until it clicks i

Magazine"

Toppi

Som

thumb will allow the slide to return forward and re-seating the round in the chamber. If the slide appears to be out of battery it may be pushed forward from the rear to seat it fully.

There are several other variations of Press Check which are taught, but the sequence above is one of the safest because it insures the trigger guard is covered with the palm of the hand and no finger can accidentally be inserted during the manipulation of the Press Check.

If you happen to accidentally eject a live round from the chamber of a semi-automatic pistol do not try to reopen the breech to replace it, this will merely cause another cartridge to eject from the breech and load the next top most round from the magazine into the chamber.

If you are wearing a holster, merely place the weapon into the holster knowing there is a live round in the chamber, press the magazine release button and remove the magazine from the butt of the gun while leaving the gun holstered.

the round in the magazine and re-
into the butt of the gun and pushing
to place. This is known as "Topping Off a

g Off.
e gun owners prefer to keep the maximum number of
und in their gun when they carry it and will Top Off a
magazine after the chamber is loaded.

Example a 1911 pistol with a full GI issue seven shot
magazine is inserted into the gun and the slide retracted and
released to strip off the top cartridge in the magazine and
load it into the chamber (set the safety to the ON position).
The magazine now only holds six rounds and the gun holds
the seventh in the chamber. You can holster or bench the
gun, remove the magazine only and Top Off one additional
round into the magazine resulting in a full seven rounds in
the magazine and one additional in the chamber or "7+1".

If this topping off technique is used, it should be used
consistently to prevent doubt about number of rounds in the
gun and magazine. If you do not use the technique every
time having one extra round to account for like the 7+1
example may be difficult to remember when reloading or
storing the gun.

If you have loaded 7+1 the magazine will appear full if
ejected. Visually confirming the full mag does not account
for the extra round in the chamber of the still live and
potentially dangerous gun.

Moreover, other people who see the apparently full
magazine may also errantly believe the gun is unloaded

(SAFETY RULE #1- **ALWAYS TREAT EVERY GUN AS IF IT IS ALWAYS LOADED!**).

Emergency Reload.
Revolver.

This type of reload is conducted when the weapon has been fired until it is empty. If you are in a gunfight and your gun is empty you are now in another emergency-you are out of ammo!

With a revolver, the normal unloading and loading sequence covered above will suffice for an emergency reload.

One tactical note applies: If you are doing an emergency reload and need to be back in battery as quickly as possible, do you have the time to reload all six cylinders? If you load only two or four cartridges and index properly so the next trigger pull brings the live round under the hammer could you be back in action that much quicker?

If you have a drop in loader, all six rounds drop in at once. If you are loading single rounds from a strip or pocket it may be more tactically advantageous to load some and put the gun back in action instead of taking the time to load all chambers.

With a revolver, do not retain the empty brass. Let it fall to the ground. Cradling the empties into your hand or pocket so you don't have to bend down to retrieve them during clean-up is a training scar you do not want to inflict on yourself.

You fight like you train. During the famous FBI Miami shoot out in 1986 with armed bank robbers, one of the agents was found to have spent revolver shell casings in his pocket and was methodically loading six rounds when a rifle armed suspect came around the vehicle and fatally shot the agent. The after action study of this gun fight changed training procedures in law enforcement all across America and the concept of loading less than six rounds into the revolver was introduced as a tactical concept.

Semi-auto.

With a semi-automatic pistol Emergency Reload, the weapon is empty and the slide will have locked automatically to the rear.

Press the magazine release button to drop the empty magazine to the ground (no attempt is made to retain this empty magazine), insert a fresh magazine. (Size of the gun can make a difference on which digit is used to press the magazine release, but using the thumb of the strong hand is generally preferred). Grasp or pinch the sides of the slide beneath the rear sight and tug the slide to the rear and let it slingshot home. If the slide does not go all the way forward, smack it sharply with the palm or heel of your weak hand to drive it into battery.

Magazine Exchange.
This reloading procedure for semi-automatic pistols is conducted after shooting has occurred and you have the time to reload safely and hopefully behind cover. The exchange part of the process involves the idea you are

154

replacing a partially empty magazine in the gun with a full magazine and are retaining the partial magazine on your person instead of letting it drop to the ground. This is of course "tactics in action" as you may need that partial mag later if you run short of ammunition again.

NOTE: Even while the exchange is in process and a magazine is out of the magazine well, the pistol still has one live round in the chamber which may be fired in an emergency before the new magazine is inserted.

When executing the magazine exchange, the quickest method is to bring the new full mag up to the butt of the gun in your weak hand, eject the partially loaded magazine into your weak hand and insert the full magazine quickly. Retain the partial load magazine in a pocket or in your waistband.

NOTE: Do not put a partially loaded magazine back into a magazine holder where your muscle memory causes you to look for full magazines.

A slower but still acceptable manner to conduct a magazine exchange is to eject the partial magazine into your weak hand then stow it in a pocket or waistband. Then grab a full magazine from a pouch and insert it into the weapon.

Shooters with small hands or those who suffer arthritis may benefit from this deliberate exchange technique when they cannot manage two magazines in one hand at the same time as listed in the variation above.

NOTE: Browning Hi-Power pistols, some Ruger pistols like the SR9 and LC9, some Smith and Wesson Firearms semi-automatic firearms to include the newest M+P pistols (but not the Shield models) may have a magazine disconnect safety which disables the trigger and renders the gun unable to fire when a magazine is removed. You should check with owner's manuals or company websites to see if you model of pistol has a magazine disconnect.

Tactical Reload.

This reloading procedure for semi-automatic pistols is conducted after shooting has occurred and once again conducted when you have the time to reload safely and hopefully behind cover. In this instance the partially loaded magazine is dropped on the ground and discarded. One round remains in the chamber during the Tactical Reload and may be fired if necessary. Inserting the full magazine immediately fully charges the weapon and no attempt is made to recover the dropped magazine.

In real life it is always a good idea to retain even partially loaded magazines, however the practicalities of doing so while moving or seeking cover with a large amount of adrenaline coursing through your veins may preclude this concept from working into your conscious brain. This again reinforces the concept that you fight like you train, and if you train yourself to retain partial magazines it may be come unconscious habit during a real iteration.

Fixing a non-firing weapon.

This is always easier to do in practice sessions! Revolvers are fairly simple machines and their fewer moving parts are inherently dependable and durable. The Ruger company was reputed to throw demonstration pistols under the wheels of large trucks and then load and fire them to show how rugged and dependable they are.

No machine is 100% dependable, but revolvers come close. One of the main reasons they would not fire following a reload is the cylinder is either not snapped all the way into the frame, or it is snapped in but the cylinder is floating and not engaged with the lock works. Bumping the cylinder in or pushing the cylinder slightly up or down may cure this issue.

The other way to prevent a revolver from firing is to assume a shooting position where the cylinder touches the wall or barricade. Thus when the trigger is pulled the cylinder cannot rotate an unfired round into position to be fired. Leaning slightly away from the wall or intrusion will free up the cylinder to rotate.

If these two situations do not put the gun back in battery immediately seek cover and retreat as necessary-there is little else you can do to fix other issues.

NOTE: If you have a revolver cylinder near a wall or your fingers are forward of the cylinders during firing sequence hot gases will expel from the front of the cylinders and scorch the surface of the wall or your fingers.

With semi-automatic pistols, 90% of the misfires involve magazines. Usually the magazine is not inserted fully, rounds are upended in the magazine or the magazine feed lips at the top are bent.

Occasionally magazine springs lose their tension and fail to raise the next round up in a timely fashion, but with high quality magazines and good springs this should not be much of an issue. Properly annealed springs should keep their pressure through thousands of rounds and even leaving them loaded for years should not result in a spring related failure to feed.

If your semi-automatic pistol fails to fire, the first action to put it back in firing order is to use the **"Immediate Action Drill"**. TAP the base of the magazine with your weak hand to insure it is seated. RACK the slide to clear the chamber of any fouled round. Release the slide so it slams home fully inserting a new round in the chamber. READY-reassess the situation-look down range and in the target area to see if it still necessary or safe to resume shooting.

This drill will clear most malfunctions (about 80% of all malfunctions) and was formerly known as TAP/RACK/BANG. It is now known as TAP/RACK/READY to build in the idea by the time you return your pistol to full function it may no longer be advisable to continue shooting.

If you conduct the TAP/RACK/READY drill and your weapon does not fire the second time you have one additional technique to try before abandoning the fight completely. After the next trigger pull does not work initiate the **Secondary Immediate Action Drill** to clear a more elaborate malfunction.

RIP the magazine out and let it fall to the ground-do not retain it as it is not considered to be faulty, WORK the slide to full extension two or three times to clear the chamber and breech area of live rounds, insert a new magazine and

TAP the base to insure it is seated, RACK the slide back and release it to slam home and READY while reassessing the shooting area to see if it is still safe or necessary to shoot.

This secondary immediate action drill was formerly known as RIP/WORK/TAP/RACK/BANG and is now known as RIP/WORK/TAP/RACK/READY.

If your Secondary Immediate Action Drill does not return the weapon to working condition seek cover and retreat if necessary. Any additional efforts to try and fix the weapon will consume more time which could be critically used to seek better cover or put distance between yourself and an attacker.

Cleaning handguns.
At the end of any range session you should clean your guns to insure they will function when called upon and also to keep a light coating of oil or lubricant on the exterior to prevent surface rust. The substances you are cleaning include lead or copper residue in the barrel, burned powder residue and even unburned powder, soot and dirty oil or grease.

Lead bullets leave the most residue in the barrel and require a solvent or product to break the melted lead loose along with scrubbing action. Copper jacketed bullets leave much less residue and do not need as much cleaning as lead.

There is an old myth that a shooter who shoots a lot of lead bullets could shoot some copper jackets at the end of the session to "clean" the lead out of the barrel. This is not true at all, the lead bullets are fired through the barrel at high speeds and the friction encountered along the barrel walls, lands and grooves scrape and melt minute traces off which fill microscopic pores. Copper jacketed ammo passing through do not act like scrubbing sponges and also leave tiny traces of their passing.

Haz-mat.

Lead and greasy oils and other deposits which foul a firearm should be treated like semi-hazardous substances. A pair of cheap latex or plastic gloves will prevent the substances from being absorbed through the skin during cleaning.

If you do not have gloves, when you are finished cleaning the weapon wash your hands with cold water and soap. Do not use hot water as that actually opens the skin pores and may allow more of the dirt and solvents to be absorbed.

Treat clothing worn on the range as contaminated and launder it separately from other household laundry if possible.

Shower and wash hair and face after a day at the range. If you have been shooting on an indoor range do not wear your shoes into your house and across carpets unless they have been cleaned.

There are huge numbers of manufacturers on the market who sell gun cleaning solvents and lubricants. They all work-some better than others, but they will all clean and protect your guns. You should have at least one solvent or degreaser and at least one lubricant to clean your guns.

Hoppes #9 is perhaps the most famous solvent and does a very good job of cleaning accumulated grease and dirt as well as lifting lead and copper deposits

Simple Green Household cleaner and degreaser works well, is very cheap by volume and non-toxic. Simple Green will degrease all metal and leave it very dry, so you will have to apply some oil or lubricant after cleaning with Simple Green.

One other point about Simple Green-it is suspended in a water base so you do need to take care to not pour it inside guns or allow it to pool. Simply soak a cotton patch or paper towel with Simple Green or other solvent and use it to rub on the dirty areas. NEVER USE GASOLINE, KEROSINE OR OTHER LOW FLASH POINT HIGHLY FLAMMABLE PRODUCTS TO CLEAN WEAPONS.

There is a long history of oils and lubricants dating back to using bear grease to prevent rust. Grease was cheap, long lasting and was used extensively in military guns as a protectant and lubricant through even the Korean War. The venerable M-1 Garand was well lubed internally with grease to keep it running smoothly.

In that timeframe, oils were lightweight films and deemed too light to be dependable. Lubrication science brought better light oils to gun owners and vehicle owners. In the late 1970's Teflon was added to oils. The Teflon products are actually microscopic round particles which filled in the microscopic pores in gun metal and reduced friction by allowing rubbing parts to actually roll over the tiny balls.

The U.S. military developed LSA oil for rifles and other weapons and remains a popular choice. It can be obtained in large volumes at very reasonable prices. LSA is a semi-fluid all weather lubricant which actually is a semi-fluid grease with a thickener. It provides lubrication and rust resistance down to sub-zero temperatures and can be both a cleaner and a lubricant.

The wars in Iraq and Afghanistan have led manufacturers to develop many excellent synthetic lubrication products, some of which are actually dry lubricants and do not leaving sticky traces which will attract sand and dirt.

You may even use synthetic motor oil like Mobil 1 as a firearm lubricant…after all, it is just an oil designed for high temperatures and extended life.

Most shooters will purchase a prepackaged cleaning kit which contains a soft aluminum cleaning rod, brushes, a patch jag, some cotton lint free patches and possibly some oil.

You can purchase the individual pieces at gun or sporting goods stores and easily replace broken or dirty individual pieces for a couple of dollars. Paper towels, shop rags and Q-tip swabs are also very handy items to have on hand.

Dabbing solvent on a patch will allow you to wipe most grime off of the gun. You don't have to soak the gun surface for more than a few seconds to lift the dirt.

Using the cleaning rod with a brass, nylon or stainless steel brush is the common manner to clean the barrel. Dampen the bore with a solvent soaked patch, run the brush through the barrel several times then run dry patches through the barrel until one comes out clean.

Cleaning the bore is simple but three cautions should be observed. If possible **always scrub from the breech to the end of the barrel-in the same path a bullet travels**.

Second, when running a brush through the barrel push it completely through-do not scrub back and forth inside the barrel-this may leave minute scratches on the lands and grooves which imparts spin to the bullets that results in a more accurate round down range.

Third, if you are using an aluminum cleaning rod be careful to not drag the rod on the inside of the barrel-the aluminum is softer than the steel barrel and may actually leave minute metal shavings in the barrel. Keep the rod centered when pushing it back and forth through the barrel.

A problem is encountered with revolvers since you cannot get a brush into the breach and scrub from the breach end in the manner that bullets travel. In that case just go from the muzzle to the breach with a cleaning rod.

There is a terrific product on the market that is now offered by at least three manufacturers which solves this problem and may replace a cleaning rod for most pistols and rifles.

Originally marketed by Hoppes, as the "Bore Snake", it is a cleaning rope with embedded bronze scrub brush in the actual rope. The Bore Snake comes in different caliber diameters and all have a weight on one end which drops a cord through the breech or chamber end of a barrel.

Solvent or oil can be applied directly to the cloth rope/snake ahead of or behind the bronze brush, then you simply pull the snake through the barrel. The amount of surface area in the snake simulates or exceeds many scrubbings with dry patches you would have to use with a cleaning rod. With modern ammunition being fairly clean burning, pulling a Bore Snake through the barrel two or three times will clean all but the most stubborn grime and it only takes a few seconds to complete.

Revolver cleaning.
No disassembly is required for routine revolver cleaning. Having the cartridges contained within the cylinder forces the bullets and most of the residues down the funnel area (forcing cone) on the beginning of the barrel and out the barrel itself. The barrel needs to be cleaned, the forcing cone and top strap of the frame. The insides of the cylinder chambers and underneath the star shaped extractor also should be cleaned and lubricated.

The outside of the revolving cylinder may exhibit back blast residue on the front facing from escaping gasses and usually in the scalloped out or fluted areas on the cylinder. This can be stubborn to remove, but do not use a brass bristle brush as it can damage the finish. Solvent soaked patches and some rubbing will eventually remove the exterior dirt.

The use of a Bore Snake works well with revolvers as it can be inserted in the forcing cone end of the barrel and pulled through in the same direction the bullet travels and can be pulled through the individual cylinders.

On occasion, a screwdriver should be used to check the snugness of screws which secure the hand grips, and your revolver may feature one or more screws holding the side plates which cover the internal lock works. Use of magnum or high velocity loads may induce screws to vibrate loose. Medium tension should be used to insure all screws are tight. Do not tighten grip screws with heavy effort as it may torque and crack the grip itself. Also, check the front and rear sights to insure they remain tight and secure with no discernable movement.

When you have finished cleaning the interior and exterior, wipe some lubricant or oil on a patch and wipe down the exterior metal for rust prevention then rub with a dry cloth to remove excess lubricant.

Semi-Auto cleaning.
Semi-auto pistols will require routine field stripping as part of their maintenance and cleaning. Field stripping involves removing simple parts like the slide, barrel, recoil rod and spring from the frame. No other disassembly is necessary for routine cleaning.

Semi-auto pistols disassemble in many different ways. Some tilt, some have disassembly levers which much be disengaged first, some have to have parts removed from the frame, and some require mechanical action to remove the slide from the frame. Every gun owner should know how to disassemble and reassemble their pistol.

Manufacturers supply owner's manuals which describe the disassembly of their gun. If you do not have one of the manuals you can contact the manufacturer and request another copy. In this age, you may also be able to find internet postings on disassembly or a video on YouTube showing disassembly you can learn from and follow along.

Another great resource is a web site which contains a huge database of owner's manuals, illustrated parts charts and Army Field Manuals. www.stevespages.com/page7.htm contains exploded parts diagrams for 68 popular pistols. It also has hundreds of pistol, rifle and shotgun owner's manuals by manufacturer from A-Z which may be accessed and downloaded. If you own a modern firearm, chances are the owner's manual is listed on www.stevespages.com/page7.htm.

Due to the presence of a recoil spring under pressure in a semi-automatic pistol, it is preferable to wear eye protection and keep the spring pointed away from you during disassembly.

Once you have the slide, barrel, recoil spring guide rod and spring removed the areas which need cleaning are fairly evident. The rails on the lower frame need to be cleaned along with the beveled front edge of the magazine well area where bullets are pushed upwards into the barrel chamber.

The slide floats along the rails when it cycles back and forth so they will need lubrication along with the rails located inside the slide. Wiping down the slide and breech is fairly easy, and the feed ramp on the barrel and barrel breech area will need cleaning as will the interior of the barrel. Since the barrel is outside of the slide it is easy to run a rod or Bore Snake through the barrel from the breech to muzzle end.

Clean the parts and the lower receiver, wipe on a coat of lubricant, and then wipe it off with a dry cloth for most pistol cleaning. Do not apply lubricant to the grip panels or into tritium or glow in the dark sights. Check the grip screws with a screwdriver to insure they are tight.

A bore light, a small flashlight, a fiber optic device or even a clean white piece of paper may be used to inspect the barrel for dirt/cleanliness on a fully assembled safe and unloaded pistol.

The white piece of paper may be inserted in the breech of the unloaded weapon and exposed to light. The light will be reflected up inside the barrel. Fiber optic devices redirect light from the breech end up the barrel as do dedicated bore lights or small flash lights. Again-the weapon must be absolutely safe and unloaded prior to this inspection.

Magazine cleaning.

Pistol magazines do not require much maintenance, but when shooting outdoors they may fall into puddles, sand, snow or mud and should be cleaned and lubricated. Most pistol magazines are made to be disassembled by the owner. Since each magazine contains a spring under tension eye protection is recommended during disassembly and re-assembly.

To take magazines apart see if the bottom floor plate slides forward off of the magazine body. Some manufacturers build in buttons or slots in their plate which acts as a tension device to hold the plate in place. You may have to use a small screw driver or punch to depress the button or slot slightly while pushing the bottom plate forward.

Be sure to capture the spring in the palm of your hand as the plate is removed or it may fling the plate or the spring itself across the room.

Disassembly Tip: You can disassemble the magazine inside a large clear plastic bag to insure the spring does not fly free.

Remove the spring and the bullet follower which sets atop of the spring and note which way it faces. Wipe down the floor plate, the spring, the bullet follower and the inside of the magazine body.

To reassemble, attach or balance the follower atop the spring and insert it all into the magazine tube, compress the spring and slide the floor plate onto the base of the magazine. Function check the assembled magazine by pushing down on the follower/spring and insure it rights itself and springs back into place.

An unusual item to be aware of with semi-automatic pistols is the fact that oils or lubricants may dry out or dissipate while the gun is being stored for a little as two months.

Different products react differently to storage conditions so it is always a good idea to inspect your semi-automatic pistol before going to the range or for carry purposes to insure lubrication is visible upon the rails.

Different gun manufacturers have widely different recommendations for internal lubrication. Of note, Glocks are recommended to have sparing use of only single drops of oil placed on the four rail guides and a drop on the cruciform. If in doubt, use very little lube on a Glock. Conversely, Sig Sauer and Beretta should have enough lubrication along the entire lower and upper rails that it should be shiny or wet and visible all along the length.

CHAPTER FOURTEEN

GUNS FOR CONCEALED CARRY.

Not everyone has the luxury of picking out an expensive firearm for concealed carry with cost being no object. Many people begin carrying guns they already own or purchasing low cost guns first.

People tend to look for smaller and smaller guns for every day carry-despite the fact they are harder to shoot accurately and not much fun to practice with due to increased recoil. Continued practice and daily carry will help sort out bad holsters, bad clothing choices and guns which are wrong for the task.

There is no perfect gun. All guns have strengths and weaknesses inherent with their design. Tradeoffs are always made for concealment vs more potent calibers in larger guns.

Shot placement remains the critical test of any shooting situation-no matter what caliber is used. People have TV or movie myths about what guns can do or how easily they kill people. Something like over 90% of people who are shot do not die. Those who do die most often have the ability to continue to fight for several seconds or minutes past the point when they were shot.

The human body is an amazingly resilient container. Unless you disrupt the brain, cause massive wounds that lead to bleeding out and rendering them unconsciousness, the body will absorb terrible wounds and continue to function. You don't have to look far into the history of modern police gunfights to find people surviving multiple hits from.45's and even shotguns.

There are myths about "Knock Down Power" in pistols and the supremacy of the .45 ACP cartridge or the .44 Magnum cartridge. Neither can hold up in the light of actual events. There is no such thing as "knock down power"-even with rifles. Look at the examples of officers or soldiers getting shot in bulletproof vests-they are not blown off their feet. Rich Davis, the president of Second Chance bulletproof vests, one of the innovators in the field, used to demonstrate his product and dispel the knockdown power myth by shooting himself in the vest in front of witnesses and cameras. The .45 ACP and even the .44 Magnum do not cause instant incapacitation or death. Shot placement makes the difference when shooting human beings.

If a gun is too large to carry and conceal you will be less likely to carry it. If a gun is too small it will be very concealable, but it may also be very difficult to shoot, may be less dependable and may not be powerful enough to disable an attacker.

Small guns usually have small sights, small sight radius and are not viable at a distance without a great deal of training and practice. Small guns may also have a lot of sharp recoil which makes shooting them unpleasant and less likely to be taken to the range for practice.

By the same token, large guns have large frames and grips and are more difficult to conceal. Larger calibers will be more powerful and have a lot of noise and recoil. Recoil can be managed by anyone, even persons of small stature if they are committed to it and train for it.

Magnum loads are very lethal, but even strong men may find shooting only one or two magnum rounds more than they want to contend with and seek out something more manageable.

Another distinct disadvantage with magnums is the strong recoil will slow down recovery and sight alignment to make a follow up shot.

When choosing a weapon for defensive carry marksmanship and competency are supreme..not caliber. Gun people have many opinions, but the tiny .22 long rifle, .25 and .32 are all too small to be counted upon to cause disabling injuries. There are many stories of .22 ammunition ricocheting around inside the human body and causing injuries with long wound tracks. This is a well-documented phenomenon, but you cannot count on a .22 to do this, it is only an occasional or unintended circumstance.

 About one third of attackers will stop their assault if shot with any caliber, and if all you have is a .22 it is better than no gun at all, but again, the tiny .22 does not routinely have enough penetration and energy to create debilitating wounds. The .22 is a great gun to learn marksmanship and pistol safety with due to light weight, nearly non-existent recoil and cheap ammunition prices, just not a good self-defense gun.

The .380 round has European roots and while it is 9mm in diameter, the casing is shorter and thus contains less gunpowder and less velocity than a 9mm. European police carried this cartridge in the mid 1900's at the same time Americans were using .38 Specials and .45 ACP's.

The .380 has reemerged in the last ten years in America as a very popular self-defense/easy to carry cartridge due mostly to the manufacture of the tiny and lightweight Ruger LCP pistol in that caliber. This tiny handgun is only 5.16 inches long, .82 inches wide and 3.6 inches tall. It can carry 6+1 of the .380 cartridges, fit in a shirt pocket, functions very dependably and sold for a modest $300-$400 price tag. A small laser was added as an option to make the gun more "shootable" and extend the effective range.

The American public flocked to this gun and bought them and ammunition up so rapidly it was difficult to find .380 ammunition on the shelf for two years. Elaborately designed hollow-point ammunition has been developed by major manufacturers to try and make this tiny gun into a viable self-defense weapon.

Taurus and Kel Tec have developed and sold similar sized .380 pistols, and in 2014 Glock introduced a downsized .380 pistol for the first time in America.

These are all very concealable guns, and better to have a gun with you when you really need one than to have a better gun at home in a safe. However, the trade off in size is offset by the less effective cartridge, shorter sighting radius, muzzle flip and amount of recoil imparted to the shooter.

Remember this .380 cartridge is nearly the same length as a 9mm Parabellum cartridge but it is being shot out of a much smaller and lighter weight gun. There is no free lunch with physics—that power and energy is felt sharply across the gun and may be described between "unpleasant" to "vicious".

As an example, the Ruger LCP weighs 8.3 ounces-while most 9mm pistols weigh three times that much. .380 is not a great choice for a first gun to learn and practice marksmanship with. Target distances should be restricted to the 7 to 10 yards.

.380 handguns are often recommended for women with the mistaken belief they will want something tiny to carry and since the gun is small it should be easy to shoot. This is bad advice. The short barrels exhibit considerable noise and muzzle flash and have recoil stronger than mid-sized firearms in 9mm or .38 Special.

There are studies which show larger recoil force is exhibited in some tiny .380s than in a full sized .45. Also, being smaller guns, if the shooter does not have a considerable amount of grip strength and experience, the gun cannot cycle correctly and may result in numerous stoppages or jams even with round nosed copper covered ammunition which is usually the easiest to cycle.

The .38 Special is a considerable step up from the .380. This round was used by military and the police through most of the 1900's. The influx of high capacity semi-autos have over shadowed this cartridge, but it remains a potent and viable self-defense round despite being limited to only five or six rounds in the cylinder.

Adding hollow point bullets can make this round more effective, but as cited elsewhere, you cannot drive a pistol bullet fast enough to guarantee hollow point expansion performance. Shot placement remains critical.

Police full size revolvers and snub nosed revolvers like the Colt Detective Special and the Smith and Wesson Chief's Special were the mainstay for .38 Special for 75 years. This cartridge is really the base line for a self-defense gun. Anything smaller, just isn't dependable or powerful enough.

Like all things American, a search went out for a more powerful cartridge than the .38 Special which ended up with the development of the .357 Magnum. The .357 is essentially a .38 diameter bullet in a slightly longer shell casing. You can put more gunpowder in the longer case and drive the same exact bullet faster and with more energy than the .38 Special.

The .357 Magnum was a huge step up in power and originally had to be housed in a large framed gun. With better engineering and metallurgy, manufacturers began making .357 revolvers on medium sized frames- the same sized frames used to make .38 Special revolvers. The Smith and Wesson Model 19 was perhaps the epitome of this iteration.

One of the best features of every .357 Magnum revolver, is the fact it can also shoot much cheaper and much less recoiling .38 Special ammunition with no modification.

Under a number of different studies, the .357 Magnum has more one shot stops of criminals than any other cartridge.

Stories of .357 Magnums cracking the engine blocks of cars or disabling vehicles remain untrue. It is a powerful cartridge in a medium framed gun, but is not magic! With the increased power also comes a resulting amount of increased vibration, noise and recoil.

Numerous manufacturers make snub nosed revolvers chambered in .357 Magnum. Anyone who has fired a .357 Magnum out of a small revolver, especially one with light weight construction of aluminum or scandium will tell you it is not a pleasurable experience. Practice sessions are loud, brief, and memorable.

During the 1980's, manufacturers developed another load in the .38 Special for law enforcement markets labelled the .38 +P. Using different powder loads, they increased the pressure and velocity of the .38 Special rounds to make them faster and have better penetration using the same .38 Special brass.

The .38 +P rounds do not reach the speed of the .357 Magnum, but they are considerably faster than a normal .38 Special round. +P ammo was quickly adopted by owners of snub nosed revolvers to have a better performing round without having to go to a magnum.

In a gun fight you probably will never notice the noise and recoil from a .357 Magnum, but the actual movement of the gun or muzzle rise in recoil would significantly delay aligning the sights for a second shot, and practicing with a .357 remains fairly unpleasant.

Next up in the line of revolver calibers, the .44 Special and the .44 Magnum rounds are well known, but less often seen as concealed carry candidates because they require a revolver with a large and robust frame to contain the power and length of the cartridge.

Like the .38 Special and .357 Magnum, you can shoot .44 Special in a .44 Magnum but cannot shoot the longer magnum in a gun designed for only .44 Special.

The recoil, noise and muzzle flash from a .44 Magnum is amazing, and quick follow up shots are just not very likely. In barrel lengths under 6" the muzzle flip is very pronounced and should be fired two handed. These guns are powerful pistols and are often used for last ditch protection in bear country, but even the powerful .44 Magnum does not approach the power of even a .30-.30 lever action rifle. The 30-30 rifle is considered to be one of the least powerful hunting rifles, and given a choice most hunters would prefer a much higher velocity rifle when hunting wild game.

Designers continued to create more powerful rounds-even more powerful than the .44 Magnum, which for many years was the most powerful handgun cartridge. Now rounds like .454 Casull, .460 Ruger and .500 S+W all have more energy and are considered to be extreme magnums housed in very large guns.

One other cartridge, the .45 Long Colt has been around since the late 1800's and was used in the iconic Colt Peacemaker cowboy style single action guns. It was a large step up from black powder guns and remains a very versatile cartridge.

Velocities are lower than a .44 Magnum, but it exhibits good foot per second speed coupled with heavy bullets. The downside is this is a long cartridge and requires a large framed gun to carry it. Gun designers moved away to smaller cartridges like the .38 Special which can be mounted in medium frame or small frame guns.

Revolvers and Revolver Manufacturers.
Smith & Wesson still make a huge variety of excellent revolvers in .38 Special, .357 Magnum and .44 Magnum. They still make the small five shot Chief's Special type of snub nosed revolvers in a number of frame metals like blued steel, aluminum, stainless steel and Scandium (ultra-light weight). They have models with concealed hammers or no hammer to avoid entanglement when drawing the gun from concealed clothing. They also make magnum versions of small guns, medium framed and large framed with similar metal constructions to make them lighter or more corrosion resistant. One even holds a unique 8 rounds.

If the hand grips do not fit to size there are a number of aftermarket manufacturers who sell grips for these guns.

The massive .44 Magnum receives the same treatments in manufacturing metals and barrel lengths and remains in high demand by gun enthusiasts. Concealment is a difficult matter for such a large framed firearm but it is a devastating pistol cartridge. The Smith & Wesson Company is well known for its excellent customer service.

The Ruger company makes a number of revolvers which are well known for robust performance. They market a snub nosed revolver, the SP 101 in .357 Magnum made of stainless steel. They have a medium sized .357 Magnum, the GP 100 with barrels in 3", 4" and 6", and the Ruger Redhawk offered in .44 Magnum and .454 Casull.

Ruger recently developed an innovative revolver, the LCR, which incorporates a polymer frame into the small gun-making it much lighter than steel or aluminum frames.

Charter Arms offers .38 Special called the "Undercover" and have a unique left handed snub nosed revolver designed for left handed shooters called the "Southpaw".

Charter Arms was quite unfortunately thrust into the limelight after David Berkowitz, the American serial killer known as "Son of Sam" used a five shot Charter Arms .44 Special Bulldog to execute his victims in New York beginning in the summer of 1976. The gun was not widely known prior to the attacks but the combination of the large cartridge with less power than a .44 Magnum made it a viable revolver. The .44 Special Bulldog was also featured in the movie "Manhunter" a prequel to "Silence of the Lambs".

Taurus is a well-known firearms company originating in Brazil. Smith & Wesson purportedly previously manufactured guns and parts in Brazil but left the country and Taurus purchased original machines to create very close copies of the S+W Chief's Special and Model 66 in stainless steel.

Taurus has evolved over the years to have a huge line of revolvers and offer them in many different colors, metals and barrel lengths. They offer small .38 Special snub nosed guns through polymer framed guns, ultra-lite frames using exotic metals, medium frames and large frames into the .44 Magnums. They even offer a revolver in 9mm. Taurus also offers a lifetime repair warranty.

Taurus has also had huge recent success with a large cylinder revolver called "The Judge". The original model was marketed and touted as a carjacking and home defense gun.

The unique feature of The Judge, is the chambers accept the powerful .45 Long Colt cartridges, .410 shotgun shot shells and .410 shotgun rifled slugs. The different loads could be intermixed in the cylinder by the loader and the shot shells turn the smooth bored pistol into a short distance shotgun.

The gun was an immediate hit with gun enthusiasts but it is quite large. Taurus followed up the success of this gun by making smaller models with shorter barrels and even polymer frames for lighter weight.

Semi Autos and Manufacturers.
The absolute king of Semi-Auto pistols for self-defense has always been the Colt .45 ACP. It was developed by John M. Browning after the American Army sought out a pistol which would work better than the .38 Special stopping attackers.

During the Philippine-American War 1899-1902, Moro guerillas were fanatical attackers who would also take drugs to stay in a frenzied state and it helped ignore wounds. The Army found the .38 Special revolvers were not satisfactory when it came to stopping these attackers. For a time the Army went back to issuing the old .45 Long Colt single action cowboy style revolvers due to the larger caliber and more powerful cartridge.

As a result of the Army solicitations for a new pistol, John Browning developed a semi-automatic pistol with the .45 ACP (Automatic Colt Pistol) cartridge and submitted it for military testing in 1910.

According to Wikipedia, one of the high points was when the Colt design ran through 6,000 rds in two days with no malfunctions. When the gun became too hot to touch it was dunked in water and firing resumed. On March 29, 1911 the U.S. Army adopted the Colt 1911 pistol. Two years later the Navy and Marine Corps adopted it as well.

The 1911 was the U.S. military sidearm from 1911 until the 1990's when it was replaced with the Beretta M9 in 9mm. With the continued wars against terrorism and guerilla actions, several elite military units have reinstituted the 1911 as their handgun of choice.

The 1911 pistol has been used and copied and modified by many different manufacturers and countries and it remains hugely successful and in demand by gun owners, competition shooters, military and law enforcement units.

Prices range from $400 for pistols imported from Philippines and Turkey to $4000 for custom built guns. It is still in service with the FBI Hostage Rescue Team, FBI SWAT units, LAPD SWAT, Army Special Forces, Marine Corps Special Operations Command and Navy SEALs.

When looking at a 1911 style pistol for self-defense and concealed carry the standard pistol may seem a bit long- about 8 inches in length with a 5 inch barrel.

The Colt Commander was developed in 1953 as a slightly smaller pistol with a 4.25 inch barrel and is about three quarters of an inch shorter than the full sized model. The Commander was introduced with an aluminum frame for lighter weight and called the Combat Commander. It still accepted the standard 7 round magazines that fit the full sized 1911.

In 1985 a compact model, the Colt Officers Model .45 ACP was marketed with a 3.5 inch barrel and shorter frame. The Officers Model holds 6 rounds of .45 ACP but will accept regular magazines which will protrude from the bottom of the pistol.

Looking at a 1911 .45ACP for self-defense you find it was originally designed to fire a 230 Grain jacketed bullet up to 950 fps. This is relatively slow compared to 9mm's or magnum cartridges, but the round has been battle proven for 103 years and the heavy bullet at 950 fps seems to deliver its energy efficiently with good penetration and leaves a large wound channel. The 1911 is very slim and easy to conceal and every holster manufacturer make many variant holsters for 1911 type pistols.

Some early drawbacks from the original designs have been addressed with more modern versions. Of note, the pistol was made to shoot full metal jacket ammunition. When using hollowpoints they may not feed reliably and cause stoppages in the feeding process. Widening and polishing the feed ramp and barrel throat can help this problem. Gunsmiths were called upon to fix many of these modifications through the years, but newer manufactured guns come from the factory with feed ramps and barrels already modified.

The other biggest problem with early guns was the sights which were very small and difficult to see. Aftermarket sights have been very popular, and again newer manufactured guns now come with bigger and better sights from the factory. The .45 ACP is inherently a very accurate round, and the addition of good sights help take advantage of this aspect.

Magazine capacity of the original 1911 was a seven round magazine-one more than a revolver. Manufacturers now sell dependable 8 round magazines and even 10 round extended magazines. There are manufacturers who market a wide bodied grip 1911 with a double stacked magazine which holds 10 and 14 rounds of .45 ACP.

Nearly every major gun manufacturer sells their own version of the 1911. Colt still sells several different models. Kimber and Springfield Armory sell a large amount of the market share of these pistols. Smith and Wesson, Sig Sauer, Ruger and Taurus also sell their own versions of these venerable firearms.

9mm progress.
The 9mm Parabellum cartridge was developed in 1902 by Georg Luger, the man who designed the famous German military Luger pistol. The term Parabellum was derived from Latin to indicate it was "for war". The 9mm did not

gain much favor in the U.S. until the 1970's, but it was used all over the world by police and military pistols and continues to be a popular chambering today. The 9mm is also the standard NATO pistol round.

After the Luger, the Walther P-38 and the Browning Hi-Power (a 13 shot semi auto designed by John M. Browning) were the next two famous pistols in WWII chambered in 9mm. Some of these made it to America, but the 9mm did not catch on in the U.S. until the Illinois State Police adopted the Smith and Wesson Model 39 in 1973-1974.

Travelling at 1200-1300 fps, the 9mm had speed a bit quicker than the .38 Special but had far more penetration, held more rounds in the magazine and could be reloaded much quicker than a revolver. Federal Agencies and police all across the nation adopted 9mm handguns as tactically superior to the .38 revolvers.

Again, similar to the history of the .38 Special, a variant +P load and a +P+ load were developed to make the 9mm even faster for law enforcement loads.

The next big 9mm advancement came in 1985 when the American military replaced the aging 1911 .45ACP frames with a new gun, the Beretta M9. The M9 is a 15 shot 9mm pistol which won an extensive competition and to this day continues as the standard pistol for all branches of the service.

Another huge change in the 9mm firearms market came in 1987 when Glock imported their polymer framed 9mm Glock 17 into America. Gaston Glock hired engineers and designers to build a pistol for Austrian Army trials and incorporated space age polymer plastic into the frame. The frame itself weighs scant ounces but is stronger by weight than steel.

The gun holds 17 rounds and its simple yet robust design won over many police and military services as well as the gun buying public. Initial claims the gun could evade x-rays were falsely made and then repeated by the media.

Glock followed the 17 up with the Model 19, a slightly smaller version which holds 15 rounds of 9mm. The Glock company aggressively marketed the pistol to American Law Enforcement and currently holds approximately 80% of the police market. The American gun buying public flocked to the Glock and it is a mainstay of self-defense minded citizens, combat shooters and target shooters.

Springfield Armory introduced a Croatian designed pistol in 2002 designated the XD. The gun was developed and competed for the Croatian Army contract and incorporated a polymer frame similar to Glock but also incorporates several ergonomic and safety changes different from the Glock. The gun has also been very well received in America with the public and with competition shooters. Springfield later developed the XDM with M standing for "Match" to upgrade their own pistol design for better ergonomics and more accuracy.

Smith and Wesson marketed a polymer framed pistol, the Sigma and later went in a joint venture with Walther to sell a polymer framed duty gun the P99. Smith currently sells a very popular polymer pistol with adjustable back straps (to fit a variety of hand sizes) the M+P (Military and Police) and has made serious inroads into the law enforcement market. Ruger, Taurus, Kahr, Kel Tec all market polymer and steel framed guns to meet the public demands for high capacity, low weight 9mms.

Sig Sauer, a West German and Swiss firm, first brought an 8 round 9mm pistol to America as the P225. Later the grip was redesigned to hold a double stacked magazine of 15 rounds of 9mm. This pistol, the P226 has a reputation for accuracy and durability and has been the frequent favorite of Navy SEAL teams and law enforcement since the 1980s.

Sig came up with a more compact model, the P228 which holds 13 rounds of 9mm. The P228 was quickly seen as a more compact pistol and was the winner of military law enforcement trials which picked the P228 (or M11 pistol) to replace the larger Beretta M9 in the concealed carry holsters of military criminal investigators from NCIS, Army CID, Air Force OSI and Coast Guard Investigative Service. Sig has also brought out a new striker fired pistol (no visible hammer) the P320 which is modular and can be owner modified to smaller and larger versions and even caliber conversions in less than a minute.

In Europe and Turkey, the 9mm continued to be used during the 1970's in many new gun designs. The CZ-75, a pistol most Americans are not familiar with, emerged from the Czech Republic. The CZ-75 is a high capacity slim 9mm pistol developed for the Czech Army. It was very accurate, dependable and had good ergonomics. This gun has been copied by many manufacturers (like EAA) and has been produced with polymer frames, multiple calibers and multiple sizes to include compact guns. Many American competition shooters use a CZ or an offshoot of the CZ-75 as their target or carry gun.

Development of the .40 S+W.
Following the famous FBI Miami Shootout, the Bureau sought out a handgun cartridge which would meet new test standards for penetration and wound channels which would be more lethal than the .38 Special and 9mm cartridges

Smith and Wesson worked in conjunction with the FBI and created an entirely new round, the 10mm. This cartridge holds a 10mm or .40 180 grain bullet and pushes it in a pistol to velocities matching or just slightly less than a .41 Magnum revolver. Glock, Kimber, Dan Wesson, EAA and others market 10mm pistols to a dedicated following of 10mm fans. Ted Nugent is a huge advocate of the 10mm as a self-defense and hunting cartridge.

The cartridge has very impressive ballistics but had to be housed in a full sized pistol as large as a .45 frame. This large frame gun and the extra recoil of a near magnum round did not fit well with smaller hands and there were some initial mechanical problems with the pistols fielded in this cartridge. The FBI went back to issuing 9mm's to their agents but continued the search for a round which would still have extra penetration and large caliber wound channel along with a medium sized gun and large capacity.

The .40 S+ W cartridges were the next step. The FBI inspired .40 cartridge, is merely a shorter version of the 10mm.

Comparatively speaking, the .40 to 10mm conversion is very similar to the .38 Special and .357 Magnum. The .40 is merely a shortened 10mm brass casing shooting the same bullet as the 10mm.

The cartridge was marketed in 1990 and Glock and Smith & Wesson were the first manufacturers to field weapons in this caliber.

The .40 touts a bullet that is significantly larger and heavier than the 9mm, but the .40 can be designed to fit in the same sized frame as 9mm guns instead of having to use larger frames like .45's and 10mm require.

The .40 cartridge is a compromise it is not as fast as a 9mm, and not as heavy or penetrate as deeply as a .45, but it is a large bullet which can be fired from a medium to small framed gun with a large magazine capacity.

The .40 reaches peak loadings at about 950 fps which is exactly the same speed as the .45 ACP, and has proven to have good penetration and wound capability similar to .45 ACP. The typical .40 bullet weighs 180 grains, the typical 9mm weighs 115 or 147 grains and the typical .45 ACP bullet weighs 230 grains.

Being a physically larger cartridge, the magazine capacity is reduced slightly from the number of 9mm rounds they can hold. For example, instead of 15 9mms in a magazine, a .40 variant may only hold 13.

Law enforcement adopted the round shortly after the FBI did, and manufacturers started offering .40 variants of their already popular guns established with the 9mm. The wide majority of American law enforcement are currently issued pistols chambered in .40 S+W.

The American gun buying public began switching to these guns after seeing them become the next major cartridge used by law enforcement. All major gun semi-automatic manufacturers now offer .40 S+W variants.

With the .40 S+W topping out at 950 fps, a later search emerged for something faster and more powerful. Sig Sauer in conjunction with Federal Ammunition brought forth the .357 Sig cartridges in 1994. The idea was to develop .357 Magnum velocities and build it into a semi-auto pistol.

The resulting cartridge looks like a .40 brass case necked down to hold a 9mm bullet. The velocities range from 1200-1500 fps, and the cartridge can be designed to fit into .40 sized guns without having to go to a larger frame.

In some cases like Glock and Sig Sauer, it is even possible to shoot .357 Sig cartridges in a .40 gun by merely replacing the barrel with a .357 Sig barrel. Since the .40 brass is the basis for the round, the regular .40 magazines will feed the new cartridge without problem.

The U.S. Secret Service and Federal Air Marshals both adopted pistols in .357 Sig. Ammunition is expensive and can be difficult to find, and despite the power of the cartridge the .357 Sig has not been a huge hit with the American public.

.45 GAP.
One additional attempt was made to create a large caliber .45 cartridge that could be fired in smaller framed guns

(similar to the 9mm/40 designs). The .45 GAP was designed in conjunction with Glock and succeeded in developing a cartridge that matched the .45 ACP ballistics and yet was able to be built into smaller framed guns. Glock markets the Glock 37 (10 rounds), the Glock 38 Compact (8 rounds) and the sub-compact Glock 39 (6 rounds).

Other manufacturers built guns for the .45 GAP, however they have all dropped them from production after the gun buying public did not pick up the idea and apparently stayed with the original .45 ACP. Glock remains the only gun maker still marketing pistols in .45 GAP.

Sub-compact pistols.
The most recent concealed carry trend in American firearms would be the concerted effort to produce 9mm, .40 and even .45 ACP pistols in sub-compact sizes which are highly sought after by concealed weapons holders as carry guns and by law enforcement for detective or back-up guns. The .380 guns have a place, but the more powerful weapons are sought out as better suited for self-defense.

The Colt Officers .45 ACP which carries 6 rounds was perhaps the first of the very small compact firearms developed from the original specifications of a large pistol. Springfield Armory, Kimber and other manufacturers offer copies of this compact .45 pistol in a 1911 frame.

In 1995 Glock introduced the Glock 26, a sub-compact 9mm pistol which carries 10 9mm cartridges. This pistol has the same deserved reputation for dependability and accuracy as the full sized Glocks.

The Glock 26 was a run-away hit with shooters looking for a very small gun that was still able to function well and still use a full sized self-defense cartridge. Glock later added a .40 S+W version, the Glock 27 which holds 9 rounds of .40 S+W.

Glock has also added compact 10mm and .45 ACP pistols in the Glock 29 and Glock 30 each holding ten cartridges, and the single stack magazine Glock 36 which holds 6 rounds of .45 ACP. These large caliber Glocks require a frame larger than a 9mm/.40, but the overall gun is considerably smaller than their full sized siblings.

Smith & Wesson have marketed sub-compact versions of their M&P pistols in 9mm and .40 and have recently added an even smaller variant called The Shield. It is less than an inch wide and has a single stacked magazine. Beretta has been offering the PX4 Storm and the six round Nano, sub-compact 9mm and .40 chambered pistols since 2011.

Ruger, in a strange reversal of gun design, took the success of their tiny LCP .380 pistol and created a larger 9mm version called the LC9 and LC9S which hold 7 rounds of the more potent 9mm cartridge.

Similarly, Kel-tec offers a 9mm version, the PF-9, which built upon success of their smaller .380 pistol. Taurus offers the Millennium Pro 111 in 9mm, a down sized version of the Millennium. Diamondback offers the single stack DB9 in 9mm. Kahr has the CM9 and CW9 pistols in their line. CZ offers the CZ 2075-a subcompact version of a CZ 75 design.

In 2014, Remington introduced the 7 shot 9mm R51. It is a modern subcompact pistol based on an old Remington Model 51 early 20th century pocket pistol design which was originally sold in .32 ACP and .380. The 2014 version is about the same size as the old Walther PPK but has upgraded features directed at concealed carry owners.

Springfield Armory offers a compact 1911 .45, but also offers variants in 9mm and .40 in the same 1911 style frame and single action trigger called the EMP. They also offer compact versions of their very popular polymer framed XD line as the XD-9 and XD-40 and a sub-compact pistol in 9mm the XD-S. One of the oft cited benefits of purchasing the XD line, is they come from the factory with multiple magazines and a polymer holster and magazine pouch.

Sig Sauer held out a long time before offering a sub-compact large caliber pistol, but in 2013 began selling the six shot P290 in 9mm. The P290 is a shortened version of the successful P228/229 pistols and has a polymer frame. They also market a sub-compact 9mm and .40 ten shot pistol in their P250 and P320 pistols.

Famous firearms instructor and gun writer Clint Smith, once said in American Handgunner Magazine; "A gun should be comforting, not comfortable". There is a lot in what he said.

CHAPTER FIFTEEN
HOLSTERS, AMMUNITION HOLDERS AND CLOTHING.

Get a holster. If you want to conceal carry then get a good holster and get one molded specifically for your gun. You may end up with several holsters before you sort out what you like or don't like, but that is OK, as you will probably learn one holster won't do everything or fit every weather situation or with all of the clothing you are wearing.

Do not buy a one size fits all model floppy nylon holster from the bargain bin. There are much closer fitting and secure holsters on the market for only a bit more money. Expect to spend more than $20 on a holster for your $500-$1000 firearm.

An open topped holster will seem to be sexy and fast, but most citizen concealed carry gun carriers should get a holster with a retaining strap or locking device if possible.

You are much less likely to lose control of the weapon or have it bounce out onto the ground at an inopportune time with a retention device (i.e. getting in and out of cars, running, bending over, stumbling, in a fight, or a vehicle crash). The time it takes to disengage a retaining strap or button to push is in the fraction of seconds and should be viewed as a minimal amount of time added to the draw, but a great benefit to every day carry and retention.

A holster with a single retaining device would be called a Level One holster. They make holsters with additional security features in Level Two and even Level Three which many police agencies use for their uniformed police holsters.

There are about as many holsters on the market as there are fishing lures on the market. Every manufacturer has different aspects to highlight from construction materials, safety features and ease of concealment.

Traditional leather holsters from cowhide, horsehide elephant, sting ray and even snake skin have a long tradition in America. Cordura Nylon, a tough abrasion resistant material was brought into the market in the 1980s, and was followed shortly thereafter by Kydex polymer plastic.

Quality leather remains the most expensive material but is usually very attractive and secure. Cordura is soft and yielding. Kydex is super strong, light weight, can be had in various colors and patterns, and is vacuum molded to the specific firearm. Most holsters can be categorized as inside the pants or outside the pants holsters.

Pancake Holster.

Some of the original highly concealable holsters the "Pancake" style are still viable as very secure and comfortable concealed carry holsters. They are called "Pancake" as they are very flat, made of two opposing pieces of leather sown together and the resulting size is similar to a pancake. Two belt loops are cut in the holster and it is threaded onto the belt and held very tight and flat up against the hip. In the 1980's Cordura Nylon was stiffened and used to make Pancake style holsters, and in the late 1900's and 2000's Kydex models were added.

Changes in the design have seen different securing devices added to hip holsters. The least secure of which is the use of a silver metal spring-steel clip on the holster. The clip is about two inches wide and slips over the waistband. It is certainly very easy to slip on and off, but it is also easy to dislodge. You may draw the gun and holster still together if the silver clip fails. Additional changes have seen the use of snaps and clips which interact more securely with a belt. This makes donning or removing the holster easier than the traditional sliding the belt through slots on the holster.

Paddle Holster.

A compromise design, the paddle holster, has become very popular in the 2000's. The idea of being able to slip the holster on and off easily without sliding it on the belt yet holding the holster and gun secure is an appealing thought.

The paddle holster has a wide Kydex curved paddle or flap riveted or screwed to the back of the holster. The paddle is tilted outward and slipped inside the waistband. Hooks on the paddle slip past the belt and secure it from inside the waistband. Many holster makers now offer their popular holsters with an optional paddle. Some will fit better than others. Some are downright uncomfortable. Recommended brand names to consider include Kydex offerings from Blade Tech, Blackhawk!, and the Israeli made Fobus line.

Fobus makes the lightest weight polymer paddle holsters (mere ounces) at a very modest price. They are molded to specific guns and are offered with and without thumb break retention straps. The Fobus paddle is very comfortable to carry all day, and it slips on and off easily.

Inside the Pants Holsters.

Inside the pants holsters slip inside the waistband and pressure from the hip against the belt helps keep it secure. The barrel of the gun is concealed inside the pants with only the handle protruding above the waistline and is thus more concealable than a pancake or paddle holster.

Cheap variants offer simple soft pieces of horsehide sewn together with a metal clip. The gun must be inserted into the holster before the entire package can be clipped inside the waistband. A problem develops when the gun is withdrawn-the soft leather collapses and the gun cannot be re-holstered without removing the holster completely from the pants. (A law enforcement saying developed around this problem saying "Take it out fast, you can always put it away slow later.")

More advanced designs (which cost more) are usually made of leather but also have a molded or stiffened band which keeps the holster from slipping shut when the gun is drawn. Re-holstering is then accomplished by digging the tip of the barrel into the holster before pushing it down.

TIP: Plan on buying pants at least one waist size bigger to compensate for the presence of the inside the waist band holster.

Inside the waistband Kydex holsters have been offered but can be less comfortable than leather or Cordura Nylon. Recent designs have created a hybrid inside the pants holster which combines leather and Kydex. A Kydex holster is attached to a wide piece of leather which slips inside the waistband. The leather molds to the wearer's hip and the also prevents the holster from being a hard unyielding lump. Some of the hybrids have clips that slip down over the outside of the waistband or have snaps or clips that fasten around the belt.

Versacarry.com hit the market in 2013 with an odd piece of plastic which is actually an inside the pants concealment "holster". It does not look like any holster you have any seen. The item is probably the lightest weight retention device on the market. It is comprised of a flat piece of black plastic that has a belt hook on one end and a colored rod on the other end.

The colored rod slides about an inch up inside the barrel of the gun and the flat plastic piece is held alongside the slide/frame of the gun. The entire assembly is inserted inside the waistline with the belt hook clipping over the waist or belt. The plastic piece rides between the skin on the hip and the side of the gun preventing chafing. There is also a rounded piece of flat plastic that bells out to cover the trigger guard.

The Versa Carry's are made for different calibers and models and are marketed for about $25. It is an innovative design which adds no bulk to carrying a concealed gun, and may be a viable option when other holsters are not going to work with the clothing or weather conditions you have available.

In hot weather it is often difficult to comfortably wear jackets or vests over belt holsters or inside the pants holsters. Fashion may also limit the untucked shirt as an option. There are a variety of alternative holsters made for deeper concealment to include inside the pocket holsters, light weight, little bulk holsters which cover a gun barrel and trigger guard while riding in large cargo pockets.

Ankle Holsters.

Ankle holsters are a well-known deep concealment option. Ankle holsters, like any other holster have their advantages and disadvantages. Advantages include the fact people don't look at your legs anticipating a handgun.

It is also possible to wear an ankle holster when it is sweltering hot and humid when you would have to wear a jacket or untucked shirt to cover a belt holster. With a bit of practice, ankle holsters can become easy to wear. At first they feel clunky like you have a large floppy weight strapped to your ankle. Wear the gun on the inside of your ankle. If it is worn on the outside edge it will extend like a spur, create a large profile, and bang into door frames and furniture.

On the down side, an ankle holster may be exposed if you tend to relax and cross your legs at either the ankle or across your knee.

The biggest tactical disadvantage to an ankle holster, is if you need to draw the gun it is very slow to engage and bending down may not be the wisest move in a violent or potentially violent encounter. Bent over is also a terrible position to try and move or defend yourself.

Many police wear ankle guns as a back-up or gun of last resort to be accessed only if their main belt gun is no longer available or viable.

If you have to draw from an ankle holster, consider going to one knee to access the gun, yank up the pant leg hem with both hands, unhook the retaining strap, draw and aim at the target from the fairly stable kneeling position instead of trying to stand immediately back up.

The kneeling position makes it difficult for you to advance, retreat or move laterally, but the amount of time involved with deploying the gun has most likely already placed you at a disadvantage and it may be better to stay low instead of just bending down and then straightening back up into the projected line of attack of your adversary.

If you decide to get an ankle holster, do not get the cheapest one you can find. Comfort will require a good design, and cheap holsters usually will not hold a gun securely and will not be comfortable. The entire holster assembly may slide around as well as ride up and down and abrading your ankle.

Tip: Forgo straight legged or tapered pants. You may get the gun under there, but it is nearly impossible to pull the pant leg up in a hurry to get the gun out. Flared leg pants or loose pant leg designs like cargo pants or Dickies style utility pants allow greater access to an ankle holster.

Shoulder Holsters.

Shoulder holsters reached a wide audience following the Dirty Harry movies and the Miami Vice TV show. Harry carried a huge 6' barreled .44 Magnum in a leather vertical holster where the barrel actually extended from the armpit to below the waistband. Detective Sonny Crockett wore a Galco leather holster with a horizontal holster which rides along the ribs and under the armpit with the barrel facing the rear. (Historical note: the actor started the series with a controversial 10mm Bren Ten pistol which Col. Jeff Cooper helped develop.)

Shoulder holsters add a lot of bulk, and must be worn with a jacket or shirt over them. Leather set ups are very exotic and attractive but can be stiff, hot and expensive. Cordura Nylon rigs are lighter, softer and less expensive.

The benefits of the shoulder holster include the fact they do well with large handguns. The down side aspects include the fact they must be covered up with extra clothing, drawing the gun from the weak side of the body takes training, and the weight and straps with extra magazines may not be worth the effort if your gun is medium to small sized and a decent belt holster is available.

Note: If you use a weak side shoulder holster on the range be cognizant of the fact when drawn the gun has to sweep in an arc behind and around you before it can arrive at a center point downrange. Do not draw the weapon with other shooters standing next to you on the holster side.

Disguised Holsters.

There have always been a market for disguised holsters, and with the popularity of the subcompact .380 pistols, several new designs have come onto the market. Some mimic the belt cell phone holders or on-the-belt camera bags. Several makers of women's purses have concealed holsters built in or concealed openings which give access to a hidden firearm.

Maxpedition.com and other bag makers sell rugged military looking gear bags and backpacks with many pockets and water bottle holders. They have shoulder straps worn looped over the neck or shoulders. Their bags usually have hidden compartments for firearms separate from main compartments and are available in many sizes and colors.

The iconic fanny pack holster has been on the market for a couple of decades now, and with most audiences it has been associated with law enforcement undercover officers long enough it now practically screams "Cop!".

There are pluses of course to any holster. The fanny pack has several. It contains an internal holster and retention strap which are very secure. It is large, has pockets and may carry other items like a small light, spare magazine or cell phone.

Best of all, the fanny pack absolutely covers the firearm at all times while strapped around your waist. You won't expose your firearm inadvertently like a belt holster or shoulder holster.

It may be too hot to wear other types of concealment clothing and a fanny pack may the only thing left that fills the bill. It is also easy to put on and take off without having to remove the firearm.

When was the last time you saw a fanny pack? On an older person? Did you make fun of it? Did you in any way suspect there might be a gun inside?

There have been refinements to fanny pack holsters to include making them much smaller and offering them in colors other than Tactical Black. A new design by 5.11. com currently markets one called the "Select Carry Pistol Pouch" which utilizes interesting designs to break up the profile of a traditional fanny pack style holster.

 The design extends the pistol barrel down the beltline and the exposed "pouch" which covers the pistol handle is a small colored square which does not look like a traditional fanny pack. Incorporating an untucked shirt, or even partially untucked shirt, will help break up the bag outline.

Deployment of a pistol from a fanny pack involves pulling zippers down and then ripping the outside of the bag open.

Tip: If you purchase a fanny pack carrier, one thing you can do to help insure a positive draw, is to attach a key fob or a small carabineer to the zipper pull tab. This allows you to visually see and physically grab the zipper tab which will allow best access to the hidden pistol.

Spare ammunition carriers.
If you carry a gun, you need to carry at least one reload of ammunition with you in case of a shooting situation. Whether you are completely empty (emergency reload) or need to top off a partial magazine (magazine exchange or tactical reload) you will need at least one loaded magazine on your person.

If your weapon jams, you may initiate the immediate reaction drill (Tap, Rack, Reassess) and if that does not work use the secondary reaction drill (Rip the magazine out, Work the action, Insert a fresh magazine, Tap the bottom of the magazine, Rack the slide, Reassess).

Dropping a spare magazine or a revolver speed loader or speed strips into a pocket will work if you have a large pocket like a suit coat pocket. Using pockets on tight fighting jeans may not work out nearly as well in a time of obvious need or emergency.

The best way to carry a reload and fastest way to reload is to utilize a dedicated magazine pouch or container on your belt. Law enforcement officers and competition shooters always carry spare ammunition in a belt mounted pouch.

Using an ammunition carrier insures the reload is going to be safely maintained in the same place every time (muscle memory), and if it is belt mounted it will be much easier to access than putting the ammo in your pocket. (Remember, spare revolver ammo is carried on the strong side of the body as the revolver ends up in the weak hand during the unloading process. Semi-auto mags are kept on the weak side of the body as the gun stays in the strong hand during reloading.)

The revolver speed loader is necessarily as big around as the cylinder it feeds into. Stuffed into blue jeans pockets they are bulky. Belt mounted carriers allow half of the bullets to straddle the top of the belt, so that makes them a bit less bulky and pretty comfortable.

Original revolver pouch holders mounted in front of the belt and protruded about two inches. The drop pouches or 2-2-2 pouches referred to previously carry six rounds of .38 Special or .357 Magnum in a small low profile leather pouch that lies flat along the front of the belt.

Speed Strips are narrow pieces of rubber or plastic which have scooped out circles which latch on to the base of revolver cartridges. When filled, the strip holds six cartridges by the bases side by side and may be used to load cylinders one or two rounds at a time by inserting the live round and pulling the strip away. The strips take up very little space and lie flat in a pocket.

Depending on movement and binding material, the act of pulling the strip out of a pocket may dislodge one or more rounds. Some old law enforcement makers in the 1950's and 1960's made leather pouches which would contain the loaded Speed Strips. Not too surprisingly, some pouches still exist today made out of more modern materials like nylon with Velcro closures. With simple internet searches you can find several Speed Strip pouches and at least one wallet that can be secured around the belt, or placed in a pocket.

Semi-automatic pistol magazines are much quicker to reload, and have the benefit of being very flat and slim. Belt pouches hold the magazine with the bottom up. (Insert the mag with bullets facing forward or the centerline-grasp the magazine between the thumb and middle finger with the index finger extended down the front spine of the magazine.) Magazine pouches should be mounted on the weak side and the pistol remains in the strong hand during reloading.

There are a large number of materials for magazine pouches, they all work, and some are more comfortable than others. Canvas, leather, Nylon and Kydex are all available. Some are made for multiple weapons (double stacked magazine pouches are commonly offered in sizes that fit several manufacturers' magazines). Prices are moderate, and well worth purchasing if you intend to routinely carry a pistol on your person.

Mag holders may be open topped or have retaining flaps. They may also be offered in outside the waistband or inside the waistband models. The belt retention device for mag pouches varies from metal clips to plastic clips, Tech-lock polymer snap together latches, belt loops and even with paddles which slip inside the waistband.

Most holster makers offer magazine pouches that match their holsters

Tip: If you use a clip-on design mag pouch do not just clip it over your belt or just over the waistband of pants worn with no belt. It can become dislodged or slide off the belt. Be sure to insert the clip over the waistband and around the back side of the belt, this way the clip is inside the band and grips the waistband and the belt as designed.)

Clothing.
Dress for concealed weapon success. Obtaining a Concealed Carry License involves a fair amount of commitment, time and money. Once you have obtained the appropriate license, the biggest mistake would be to use

your gun inappropriately. The second biggest mistake would be to expose your weapon to the public inadvertently.

Unintended exposure negates the tactical advantage of being able to carry a gun in the first place, and may draw public or unwanted police attention to you. Careful consideration of clothing, holsters and size of firearm will all contribute to your gun remaining concealed at all times.

On the plus side, you do not have to eliminate every bulge and corner to be concealed, and luckily most people in America are too self-absorbed to focus on other human beings.

It is more likely you will be the one exposing the gun as opposed to someone spotting it. By dressing poorly, or failing to recognize you are not well concealed, you are likely to show a pronounced imprint noticeable by others.

You must self-critique your concealment carry modes, and be honest with yourself about it. Use a mirror and heed the image. Alternatively, have a spouse or friend look and see if they can spot your firearm when you believe you are fully concealed.

Shirts.

The good old American untucked T-shirt is the most likely of all your clothing to expose your gun or show a gun outline imprint. T-shirts simply may not be long enough to cover your gun and holster fully. The shirts have a tendency to ride up with movement like exiting a vehicle or stretching. Exposing your gun and getting spotted via a wardrobe malfunction is a definite bad day.

The tail of a favorite T-shirt may also be too short, and when you bend or reach up the tail may ride up and expose your pistol. Another T-shirt issue, is some shirts are very thin material and get thinner over time when laundered and become somewhat see through. Some shirts will also exhibit significant shrinkage in the first washing and drying cycle.

Tight fitting T-shirts will cling to the holster/gun outline quite successfully. Place yourself in the mind of your average citizen. It is always a bit of a shock to see a gun imprint on a person when you are out in public. Your first thought will always be, "That man has a gun!" followed by "Am I in danger?" Your first thought will never be "They must have completed the Illinois 16 hour training course and paid a large amount of money to the trainer and to the state to obtain a license so they can become a legal concealed carry citizen who is obeying all applicable state and federal laws."

If you insist on using a T-shirt for concealed carry it is recommended you obtain shirts that are one size larger than you would usually wear. They look baggy, yet those extra inches of material can create rolls and folds beneficial to you.

Also, the T-shirt tail will be longer and help with the bending/stretching movements. A colored or patterned shirt will generally conceal better than a white t-shirt.

Wearing another untucked shirt like a button down shirt over a T-shirt is always preferable to just the T-shirt alone. The over shirt can be buttoned or unbuttoned. In the unbuttoned version the shirt will fall away from the centerline and naturally bunch up near the hips like drapes-which incidentally help cover your concealed weapon.

5.11. com, Woolrich, Blackhawk and others dealers market "tactical" concealed firearm friendly shirts which address most of the shortcomings of the T-shirt. These specialty shirts are generously cut to avoid imprinting over the hips.

The hems are square cut, so they do not look unusual if worn untucked. They also have snaps or pull away Velcro tabs holding the shirt together which can be yanked back to expose the handgrip of a pistol. They may also have a stiffener or extra mesh in the hip area which helps keep the material from clinging or imprinting the weapon.

Pants.

Similarly, concealment friendly pants are offered. They run the gamut from cargo pants to dress pants to jeans. Totersjeans.com offer blue jeans created by Blackie Collins a very well-known custom knife and holster designer.

The jeans have extended lined pockets which work as pocket holsters. The pockets are lined with Cordura Nylon to avoid imprinting and to avoid wear and tear on the pocket lining.

CCWbreakaways.com offer cargo pants and jeans which allow the pistol to be holstered inside a flap or pocket of the pants and the flap/pocket is secured over the top with a snap or Velcro. The user inserts their hand into the pocket and pops the flap outward to draw the gun from concealment. 511.com and Blackhawk offer other concealment pants.

Vests.

Vests are a great compromise in concealing a holstered weapon. They add an extra layer of concealment, usually have pockets over the areas where a weapon would bulge, generally have a loose fit, and should have long tails. Some of the original vest carry of firearms goes back to black powder days and through cowboy and riverboat gambler days with derringers tucked into vest pockets.

Leather vests are still being made which not only cover a holstered weapon; they may have holster pockets designed inside the actual vests. These vests may be found in western/cowboy motif or in motorcycle styles.

The biggest design change for concealed carry vests came some 20 years ago when gun toters discovered the Royal Robbins vest. Royal Robbins sold rugged vests and cargo type pants to rock climbers and outdoors enthusiasts. The Royal Robbins style vest is familiar to everyone who has ever seen a "Safari Vest" in an airport or a "Photographer Vest" at a televised sporting event.

The difference with the Royal Robbins style is these vests are more durable, have better cloth and are much longer than fly fishing or Ranger Vests. They have big hip length flap pockets, many other cargo pockets and zippers. They will absolutely cover a hip holstered weapon and have many additional pockets for spare ammunition, flashlights etc.

Royal Robins later worked with 5.11 and added hidden pull apart pockets inside the vest designed to carry firearms in holsters Velcro-ed to the lining. An entire line of accessory products were marketed to carry handcuffs, magazine pouches etc in the hidden pockets.

This style of vest became very popular with bodyguards and military forces during the Iraq war. You could easily conceal a pistol without the addition of a full jacket in a warm climate. The many pockets made them ideal for travel and other outdoor and law enforcement activities.

Unfortunately, the extensive use of these vests has been seen so often on television, they now may trigger a "Man hiding a gun" response.

If you are wearing the vest, most people are not interested enough in you to worry about it, but there is an increasing percentage that may see it as an aggressive visual sign you are carrying a weapon. This may be completely agreeable to you, but be honest in your self-evaluation of what you look like in such a vest.

There are other non-safari more covert vests on the market which are less obvious. If interested, you can look at biking and jogger's vests made from polyester or cotton blends from sporting goods manufacturers like Nike, Gold's Gym, and Columbia etc. You can also look at golf vests, which tend to be long tailed and made in bright colors.

Polar Fleece vests are excellent for concealed carry. The thickness of the fleece and the bulky or loose cut helps the vest drape across the body without clinging or printing.

Polar fleece vests are available for $10-$50 and come in a wide variety of colors. They can be purchased at most retail and discount stores to include Wal-Mart, Target and most sporting goods stores. The only drawback for Polar Fleece is of course it cannot be worn well in warm climates. Eddie Bauer and Blackhawk sell 200 weight fleece which is fairly light weight, but even that is not comfortable most places when the temperature goes over 70 degrees. Several manufacturers like 511.com are now selling Polar Fleece jackets with hidden holsters or pass through pockets to enhance concealed weapon carry.

Another source for vests and concealment clothing is Scottevest.com. This company designs and builds ordinary looking clothing with multiple hidden pockets to hide passports, money, sunglasses etc and most have cord channels to slide in earphone cords for MP3 players or cellphones.

Their signature vest has 24 different pockets built in. They also make light weight spring weight jackets and Polar Fleece jackets, pull overs and hoodies. Scottetvest.com also offers garments specifically designed for women.

Jackets.

BassProShop.com is currently selling a hoodie called the "Propper Cover CCW for Men" which has a hidden kangaroo pocket secured with a magnet which allows covert draw from inside the sweatshirt.

Light weight jackets are great cover ups, and during the winter months you need only to look at the people around you to see how popular Polar Fleece jackets are. They will provide warmth over a wide temperature range and breathe well. They make great concealment garments if the tail is long enough. Try to choose colors other than Tactical Black.

Another lightweight jacket that works very well are military BDU shirts. They can be found in many camouflage prints (both military and commercial) and can be had in plain colors as well.

The BDU shirt is by design very long tailed and has large cargo pockets on the front which help conceal any bulk underneath. They are made of a variety of materials to include Rip-Stop Nylon and other blends which may include light weight/hot weather materials.

Sport Coats have the necessary length and thickness to cover well and have internal and external pockets for accessories. They are also welcome at almost any occasion even with blue jeans. With this heavier material, drawing from a hip holster may require a vigorous shove of the jacket out of the way before the strong hand can grip the pistol. Some practitioners carry car keys or some small weighted items in the strong side coat pocket to insure the coat tail flies to the rear long enough to allow access to the pistol.

Belts.

Quality belts can also assist with comfort and support for concealed carry. Ordinary belts may lack the stiffness to take the additional weight of a pistol and holster hung from the outside.

One of the "tells" for concealed carry is someone who gets out of their car and then has to hitch up their pistol and belt, or they have to keep pulling up their pants waistband as they walk because their belt cannot hold the pants up.

Numerous manufacturers offer belts specifically designed to be thicker and stiffer construction than ordinary belts, and may actually have a plastic insert running through the belt to insure stiffness.

These belts can be purchased in both jeans width and dress belt widths in a wide variety of colors, materials and patterns without looking like cowboy or gun belts.

They obviously cost more than a normal belt, but they will last for years and do a much better job of securing your weapon. Bullhidebelts.com, 511.com, Amazon.com, Midwayusa.com and Cabelas.com all offer gun designed belts.

CHAPTER SIXTEEN
STATE AND FEDERAL LAWS.

United States Constitution

Second Amendment

A well regulated Militia, being necessary to the security of a free State, the right of the people to keep and bear Arms, shall not be infringed.

United States Code

18 U.S.C. § 930(a) an individual is prohibited from possessing or attempting to possess a firearm in a federal facility, which is broadly defined in the statute to include "a building or part thereof owned or leased by the federal government, where federal employees are regularly present for the purpose of performing their official duties."

Some exemptions allow individuals with a state-issued License to carry concealed firearms in federal park lands (36 C.F.R. §§ 2.4(e) & (h), 18 U.S.C. § 922(q)) allow for individuals carrying concealed in accordance with the laws of the state in which the federal park is located to carry concealed in them. Check with each Federal Park or forest service before setting out for those locations and follow all posted regulations.

26 U.S.C. § 5801 through 26 U.S.C. § 5872. Known as the National Firearms Act (NFA), which is listed under the Internal Revenue Code was passed in 1934 and instituted a tax on the manufacture of Title II firearms and federal registration of firearms. In 1968 the Act was added to by the 1968 Gun Control Act which stopped import of non-sporting firearms like small cheaply made pistols.

Illinois State Laws

430 ILCS 65 The Firearm Owner's Identification Act

430 ILCS 66 The Firearm Concealed Carry Act

430 ILCS 66/70 Violations
(b) A CCW license will be suspended if an order of protection is granted against a license holder.
(d) a CCW license holder shall not carry a firearm while under the influence of alcohol, drugs for intoxicating compounds. 1st and 2nd offenses are Class A misdemeanors. A 3rd offense is a Class 4 felony.

Criminal Offenses
720 ILCS 5/ Criminal Code of 1961.
720 ILCS 5/Art. 7 Justifiable Use Of Force; Exoneration
Sec. 7-1. Use of force in defense of person.
Sec. 7-2. Use of force in defense of dwelling.
Sec. 7-3. Use of force in defense of other property.
Sec. 7-4. Use of force by aggressor.
Sec. 7-5. Peace officer's use of force in making arrest.
Sec. 7-6. Private person's use of force in making arrest.
Sec. 7-7. Private person's use of force in resisting arrest.

Sec. 7-8. Force likely to cause death or great bodily harm.

Sec. 7-9. Use of force to prevent escape.

Sec. 7-11. Compulsion.

Sec. 7-12. Entrapment.

Sec. 7-13. Necessity.

Sec. 7-14. Affirmative defense.

720 ILCS 5/24 Illinois firearm laws and crimes (et al)
720 ILCS 5/24-9 Firearms: Child Protection

720 ILCS 5/24-1. UNLAWFUL USE OF WEAPONS
Sec. 5/24-1.2. Aggravated discharge of a firearm.
Fired towards occupied building/vehicle/peace
officer/police vehicle/EMT, Teacher or Emergency Worker
or vehicle (firemen). Class X and Class 1 felonies.

Sec. 24-1.2-5. Aggravated discharge of a machine gun or a
firearm equipped with a device designed or used for
silencing the report of a firearm. Class X Felony.

Sec. 24-1.5. Reckless discharge of a firearm.
Endangers others. Also a passenger shooting from moving
vehicle. Class 4 felonies

Sec. 24-1.6. Aggravated unlawful use of a weapon
Public carry of loaded, uncased gun, stun gun or taser.
Ammunition accessible, No FOID card or CCL, previous
Delinquent, previous drug offender, subject of an order of
protection in the last 2 years, carrying during violent
misdemeanor, minor under 21 possessing/using firearm.

Sec. 24-1.8. Unlawful possession of a firearm by a street
gang member.

Sec. 24-2.1. Unlawful use of firearm projectiles.
Manufacture, sell, purchase, possess, carry armor piercing shells, dragon breath shotgun shells (emits fire), bolo shotgun shells (2 or more stringed balls connected by wire) or flechette shells (2 or more winged projectiles). Class 3 felony.

Sec. 24-2.2. Manufacture, sale or transfer of armor piercing bullets, dragon's breath shells, bolo shells, or flechette. Class 4 felony.

Sec. 24-3. Unlawful sale or delivery of firearms.
Sale or delivery to: minor under 18, under 21 with a criminal record, narcotics addicts, convicted felons, mental institution patient (within 5 yrs), 72 hr waiting period for handguns, 24 hr waiting period for long guns, under age 18 without a FOID card, person who does not display FOID during transfer or sale. Class X, 1, 2, 3, and 4 felonies.

Sec. 24-3A. Gunrunning.
Sells or transfers three or more weapons in unlawful sales or deliveries. Class X and Class 1 felonies.

Sec. 24-3B. Firearms trafficking
Person without FOID card who brings/transfers/sells guns or ammunition into the state with intent. Class X and Class 1 felonies.

Sec. 24-3.1. Unlawful possession of firearms and firearm ammunition
Possession of concealable weapon or firearm while under age 18, possession under 21 with a criminal history, possession by narcotic addict, mental health institution

resident (last 5 yrs), intellectual disability, possession of explosive bullet. Class 4 Felony and Class A Misdemeanor.

Sec. 24-3.2. Unlawful discharge of firearm projectiles
Use of armor piercing, dragon's breath shells, bolo shells, or flechette. Class X and Class 2 felony.

Sec. 24-3.3. Unlawful Sale or Delivery of Firearms on the Premises of Any School. Class 3 felony.

Sec. 24-3.5. Unlawful purchase of a firearm.
Misuse or hiding identity during purchase or intent to purchase and deliver to another prevented at law from possessing weapon. Class X, 1 and 2 felonies.

Sec. 24-3.6. Unlawful use of a firearm in the shape of a wireless telephone. Class 4 felony.

Sec. 24-3.7. Use of a stolen firearm in the commission of an offense. Class 2 felony.

Sec. 24-3.8. Possession of a stolen firearm. Class 2 felony.

Sec. 24-3.9. Aggravated possession of a stolen firearm.
Person not entitled to a firearm, knowingly had 2-5 guns in 1yr, 6-10 guns in 2 yrs, 11-20 guns in 3 yrs, 21-30 guns in 4 yrs, more than 30 guns in five years. Class 1, 2 and X felonies.

Sec. 24-4.1. Report of lost or stolen firearms.
Gun owner MUST report theft/loss to police within 72 hours of occurrence. Class A misdemeanor.

Sec. 24-5. Defacing identification marks of firearms
Alter, remove or possess gun with serial no./manufacturer numbers altered or removed. Class 3 felony.

Sec. 24-9. Firearms Child Protection

Unlawful to leave firearm unlocked or unattended in area where minor under 14 is likely to gain unsupervised access and minor causes death or great bodily harm. Class C misdemeanor. Exception- if gun was secured with device, was left in a locked container or was in an location not accessible to a minor under the age of 14.

Sec 24-9.5 Handgun Safety Devices.

Federal Firearms License dealers must provide at key or lock which will render pistol inoperable with any new firearm sale.

CHAPTER SEVENTEEN
STATES WHO RECOGNIZE THE ILLINOIS CONCEALED CARRY LICENSE.

With Illinois being the last state to recognize Concealed Carry, they also previously never recognized any other state's Concealed Carry License holders to carry a gun in Illinois.

There is no universal recognition of Concealed Carry Licenses between states. A "reciprocal agreement" between states means the two states will recognize each other's carry license process and allow concealed carry while visiting in the state. Unfortunately, since Illinois never recognized other states' rights before now, few states recognize the Illinois license as being valid outside Illinois and Illinois never intended the license to be used outside the state.

WARNING: You are responsible for obeying and knowing the laws of any state other than Illinois where you intend to carry a concealed weapon. The laws are subject to change and it is advisable to contact local attorneys, police or obtain lists and books which contain the various state laws or check current status via the internet or the NRA.

The information listed below is not a restatement of the law or any guarantee how an Illinois resident will be treated out of state-

As of January 2017, twenty six states may recognize Illinois CC Licenses for Illinois residents travelling through those states. (Note: State laws are subject to frequent change and should always be researched before travelling to those states with an intent to carry concealed firearm with the hope an Illinois Concealed Carry License will be recognized and allow such carry in the other state).

According to www.usacarry.com in 2017, the following states may honor the Illinois Concealed Carry License: Alabama, Arizona, Arkansas, Idaho, Idaho, Indiana, Iowa, Kansas, Kentucky, Michigan, Minnesota, Mississippi, Missouri, Montana, Nebraska, Nevada, North Carolina, Ohio, Oklahoma, South Dakota, Tennessee, Texas, Utah, Vermont, Virginia, Wisconsin are the states which may allow Illinois Concealed Carry License holders to travel armed in their state.

Additional internet resources for researching up to date Concealed Carry License reciprocity by other states are listed below:

www.Youcancarry.com
www.USAcarry.com
www.CCWbystate.com
www.Handgunlaw.com
www.ConcealedcarryHQ.net

SMART PHONE RESOURCES.
Smart phone apps are also available via iTunes and the Google Play Store which can be installed on smartphones and tablets which list up to date profiles on state concealed carry laws and state reciprocity maps and may be the very handiest way to check the laws in states you may be

travelling to or through and some of the cheapest insurance to avoid a legal entanglement.

Here are a list of some of popular App's:

Concealed Carry 50 States.   Charge .50

Concealed Carry News   Free

Concealed Carry Handguns   Free

Legal Heat   Charge .99

CCW Laws-Concealed Carry Charge .99

CCW Laws Concealed Carry Guns Charge $1.49

Posted! Carry List Anti Gun   Charge .99
(lists hotels and business locations known to prohibit Concealed Carry on the premises)

Carry Alerts   Charge $2.99
(monitors your location and notifies when you are near posted anti-gun zones)

Concealed Carry   Charge $2.99

CCW USA   Charge $1.99
(notifies you if you cross into a non-reciprocal state)

CHAPTER EIGHTEEN
APPLYING FOR THE ILLINOIS CONCEALED CARRY LICENSE.

There are a number of steps involved with applying for and successfully obtaining the Illinois Concealed Carry License. Many people mistakenly believe all they have to do is undergo the mandatory training and the License will then be issued. This is not correct. A very specific process must be followed by the applicant to the Illinois State Police in order to receive a license. The web based process was somewhat unwieldy when it was first instituted, but in the intervening two years has been made somewhat more user friendly.

The authoritative source for all of the necessary information and application process is listed on the Illinois State Police web page www.isp.state.il.us. Once the web page is accessed, on the left side of the page click on "Firearms" and then "Concealed Carry"

BEST GUIDE TO THE APPLICATION PROCESS.
The application process is very detail specific and has caused frustration to many applicants since the 2014 inception. There is a new 26 page PDF file "Go-by Guide" with step by step instructions on the ISP website. It is found on the Frequently Asked Questions page.
https://www.ispfsb.com/Public/Faq.aspx

Click "Assistance to the public" and then Click "Steps to the Application Process" and finally "Click here to view

step by step instructions on how to apply for a Concealed Carry License."
https://ispfsb.com/Public/Firearms/CCLOverview.pdf

The PDF file lays out step by step instructions and shows each fill-in-the-blank box you will encounter in the application process. It is highly recommended an applicant print a copy of the PDF file to ease their way through the online application process.

You will also register for an Illinois State Police User ID through the ISP website which you can use to re-access the site in case you did not get your application 100% completed or if it is rejected for any reason.
https://www.ispfsb.com/Public/login.aspx

On the Concealed Carry page you can check your eligibility and see a checklist of requirements and look up an authorized instructor in your area.
https://cc14illinois.com/ccw/public/home.aspx The instructor data base is searchable by County, City or Last name of the instructor. Instructor name, street and city address, county, telephone and email information are all listed in the database.

ITEMS NECESSARY TO SUBMIT A SUCCESSFUL CONCEALED CARRY LICENSE APPLICATION.

Find an eligible instructor in your area pay their fee and take the training. Upon successful completion you will be issued an Illinois State Police (ISP) "Concealed Carry Firearm Training Certificate" which will have the instructor's ID number and the course curriculum ID. The certificate will need to be scanned into a computer and as an attachment to the final License application.

The Concealed Carry course is a state mandated 16 hours, however some credit can be extended for prior training. 4 hours credit may be applied for previous completion of Illinois Hunter Safety Course, Utah Concealed Carry class, Florida Concealed Carry class, Nevada Concealed Carry class, Missouri Concealed Carry class, Kentucky Concealed Carry class, Michigan Concealed Carry class and Chicago Firearms Safety Course.

8 hours credit may be applied for previous completion of NRA Basic Pistol, NRA Personal Protection in the Home, NRA Personal Protection Outside the Home, Active, Retired or Honorably Discharged member of the U.S. Armed Forces, and a previously qualified law enforcement or corrections officer under 430 Illinois Compiled Statutes Section 75(j).

You must have digital fingerprints (Live Scan) taken and have them submitted. On the ISP Concealed Carry web page, https://cc14illinois.com/ccw/public/home.aspx there is a button to assist patrons locating Live Scan providers in their area. The button leads to a database which lists vendors who will take digital fingerprints and transmit them to the ISP. Note: Applicants cannot submit their own prints or have a police agency scan their prints. They must use a state certified vendor. The vendors have a scanner which is linked to a computer and sends the prints digitally to the state police. Applicants place their fingers on a special scanner screen, and the prints are captured digitally and transmitted to the Illinois State Police database. The vendor will provide the applicant with a TCN number-this is the storage code associated with the applicant's fingerprints and the TCN will have to be entered by the applicant onto the final application for the Concealed Carry License.

An applicant can opt-out of the live-scan fingerprinting and submit his/her Illinois CCL application without paying for the private fingerprinting – but this will automatically cause a delay in CCL License approval. The state will have to conduct a manual search for fingerprints and advises this will absolutely delay the CCL application process. Submitting your application without the digital prints may be $60 cheaper, but may take up to 120 days to process instead of up to a 90 day process with the digital prints on file.

Illinois State Police User ID. The applicant must have or obtain an Illinois State Police User ID which is issued by the state. To obtain the necessary ID obtain it from the ISP Concealed Carry webpage, https://www.ispfsb.com/Public/login.aspx

Illinois State FOID Card. Applicant must have a valid Illinois State Firearms Owners Identification Card (FOID) to apply for a CC License. The application process is once again fully described on the Illinois State Police web page, http://www.isp.state.il.us/ under the "Firearms" button on the left hand side of the page and then select FOID for a menu of what the card is, how to apply for it and the form necessary to do so. There is a fee of $10 (by check or money order) and the card is valid for ten years. The FOID process is run by the ISP, has received record numbers of requests since 2012, and may take several weeks to process.

A recent photograph. A photo of face neck and shoulders taken within the last 30 days will need to be scanned and attached to the application form. This is uploaded to the application itself. Once you have a photo on your computer, just click on "Browse" and go to that picture file and then have it upload into the application

Residency. Applicant must be able to prove their last 10 years of residency. You must fill out your current address and click "Add address" to add blanks for the next most recent addresses. The dates must match up and the blanks also require the county for each address be listed as well as the street and city address.

Fee for CC License. The state requires a fee of $150. The state by law will issue or deny the License within 90 days. If the applicant does not have a TCN number for fingerprints on file a manual search will be conducted by the ISP and up to 30 additional days are granted for the final disposition of the application. The License is valid for five years and renewal fee is $15.

BIBLIOGRAPHY

Barrett, Paul M. "Glock. The Rise of America's Gun"
NY, NY: Broadway Paperbacks 2013

Cirillo, Jim, "Guns, Bullets and Gunfights- Lessons from a
Modern Day Gunfighter." Boulder Co: Paladin Press
Enterprises, Inc. 1996

Clinton, Paul, "5 Gunfights That Changed Law
Enforcement."
http://www.policemag.com/channel/patrol/articles/2011/05/
5-gunfights-that-changed-law-enforcement.aspx 05 May,
2011.

Cooper, Jeff, "Principles of Personal Defense."
Boulder CO: Paladin Press 2006

Cunningham, Eugene, "Triggernometry. A Gallery of
Gunfighters" Barnes and Noble Books 1969

Gottlieb, Alan and Workman, Dave, "Shooting Blanks.
Facts Don't Matter to the Gun Ban Crowd." Bellevue, WA:
Merrill Press 2011

Grossman, David, "On Combat, The Psychology and
Physiology of Deadly Conflict in War and Peace. " Warrior
Science Publications 3rd Edition 2008

Grossman, David, "On Killing: The Psychological Cost of
Learning to Kill in War and Society."
Back Bay Books Revised Edition 2009

Keleher, Mike, "Concealed Carry Basics-Illinois Concealed Carry Training Companion." Black Rifle Ranch Publishing, www.lulu.com 2014

Kirchner, Paul, "Jim Cirillo's Tales of the Stakeout Squad." Boulder Co: Paladin Press 2008

Lake, Stuart N. "Wyatt Earp. Frontier Marshal" NY, NY Pocket Books 1994

Leggero, Brian, "Concealed Carry Illinois Handbook" Rockford, IL: Brian Leggero 2014

Lott, John, "More Guns, Less Crime. Understanding Crime and Gun Control Laws" Chicago, IL: University of Chicago Press 3rd Edition 2013

Price. L & Welsch, "Illinois Concealed Carry Reference Guide" El Paso, IL: Ethos Tactical L.L.C. 2014

Nonte, George C. "Firearms Encyclopedia" NY, NY: Outdoor Life /Popular Science Publishing Co. Inc. 1973

Rosa, Joseph G. "The Gunfighter. Man or Myth?" Norman, OK: University of Oklahoma Press 1969

Shaw, John and Bane, Michael, "You Can't Miss" 2nd Edition, Memphis,TN: Shaw/Bane Publishing 1985

Shaw, John and Currie, Bill, "Shoot to Win" Memphis, TN: Mid South Institute of Self Defense 1985

Shooter's Bible 103rd Edition NY, NY: Skyhorse Publishing 2011

Stephens, John Richard, "Wyatt Earp Speaks!"
NY, NY: Fall River Press 2009

RECOMMENDED READING

American Handgunner Magazine
FMG Publications, also Americanhandgunner.com
 Monthly magazine featuring outstanding gun writers Clint
Smith, Massad Ayoob and John Connor. One year
subscription $19.75, American Handgunner, PO Box
509093, San Diego CA 92150-9829

Ayoob, Massad F. "In the Gravest Extreme: The Roles of
the Firearm in Personal Protection."
Police Bookshelf 1980

Ayoob, Massad F. "The Truth About Self-Protection"
New York, NY: Bantam Books 2004

Lott, John, "The War on Guns"
Chicago, IL: University of Chicago Press 2016

"GunNews" newspaper featuring Illinois based gun and
CCW law news www.gunsavelife.com. Yearly membership
$30- GunSaveLife.com, PO Box 51, Savoy, IL 61874

Jordan, Bill, "No Second Place Winner."
Police Bookshelf: English Language Edition 2013

Made in the USA
Lexington, KY
26 November 2017